美味小菜
APPETIZERS
CHINESE STYLE

作　　　者	林麗華
翻 譯 顧 問	葛潔輝
出 　版　 者	純青出版社有限公司
	台北市松江路125號4樓
	郵政劃撥12106299
	電話：(02)25084331・25074902
著作財產權人	財團法人味全文化教育基金會
版 權 所 有	局版台業字第3884號
	中華民國85年5月初版發行
	中華民國88年1月二版發行
印　　　刷	中華彩色印刷股份有限公司
定　　　價	新台幣參佰元整

Author	Lee Hwa Lin
Translation Consultant	Connie Wolhardt
Publisher	Chin Chin Publishing Co., Ltd.
	4th fl., 125, Sung Chiang Rd.,
	Taipei, Taiwan, R.O.C.
	Tel:(02)25084331・25074902
Distributor	Wei-Chuan Publishing
	1455 Monterey Pass Rd., #110
	Monterey Park, CA91754, U.S.A.
	Tel :(323)2613880・2613878
	Fax:(323)2613299
Printer	China Color Printing Co.,Inc.
	Printed in Taiwan, R.O.C.
Copyright　Holder	Copyright© 1996
	By Wei-Chuan Cultural-Educational Foundation
	First Printing, May, 1996
	Second Printing, Jan., 1999
	ISBN 0-941676-69-2

序

在一般人傳統觀念裡，認為中式小菜（或稱冷盤、前菜）不如西餐的開胃菜精緻，侷限在海鮮、豆干、小魚干和滷味等簡單菜色，變不出新鮮花樣，色彩也不如西餐開胃菜鮮美，以至於餐廳吃飯時，只會從現成擺出來的菜餚裡，任選幾樣當作飯前小菜。這種惡性循環，使中式小菜的樣式、設計與西餐相比，相形遜色。

事實上，中式小菜的格局可以擴大些，掌握小菜的精神應是關鍵，它的最大特色是事前烹煮、調味及入口的新鮮度。以涼拌菜而言，必須特別注意材料的衛生與鮮美，因為涼拌菜多半未經烹煮或是煮熟後調味再冷食，處理過程中的衛生與否是絕對條件。

當然，中式小菜的樣式繁多，絕不止於冷盤、涼拌，而是冷熱俱全。我們幾經研發與搜尋，極盡心力的設計出９２道精緻小菜，綜合各家特色，調理出色香味俱全的佳餚，而這些小菜在口味上並不遜於大菜，有些也可當成家常菜，增加飯桌上的豐富性。

Foreword

Chinese appetizers, also called cold platters, offer delectable taste experiences for those who wish to sample unique Asian hors d'oeuvres which will delight their palate. The expert use of limited ingredients such as various seafoods, pressed bean curd, dried small fish and other simple braised soy foods assure the diner of gastronomical pleasure.

Although limited in ingredients, the variety and scope of chinese appetizers can be extended by embracing their "Appetizing Spirit". This "spirit" means that any dish can be made into a tasty appetizer if prepared before hand and special seasonings are used. For the cold mixed dishes (salads), sanitary conditions and freshness of ingredients are crucial.

With the new recipes presented in this book, appetizers are not just limited to cold mixed dish platters. Through painstaking research, we have created 92 fine and delicate recipes which combine the unique regional flavors of various chinese provinces. In addition, many of these dishes may also be served as a main course, further augmenting the reader's choices for home cooked meals.

Lee Hwa Lin

目錄 · Contents

豬、牛肉類 · Pork & Beef

雞鴨類 · Chicken & Duck

特殊材料的介紹 · Introduction of Special Ingredients

紅糟 · red fermented wine rice

箭筍 · small bamboo shoot

綠竹筍 · fresh bamboo shoot

桂竹筍 · boiled long bamboo shoot

烤麩 · bran puffs

紅糟腐乳 · preserved red bean curd

辣油 · chili oil

洋地瓜 · jicama

 乾辣椒 · dried red chili pepper

 白豆乾 · white pressed bean curd

 小茴 · fennel

 桂皮 · cinnamon

 粉皮捲 · mung bean sheets

 黃雪菜 · yellow pickled mustard greens

 豆包 · bean curd pouches

 沙薑 · sand ginger

九層塔 · basil

豆豉 · fermented black beans

大頭菜 · Chinese turnip

香菜 · coriander

花枝 · cuttlefish

透抽 · squid

中式火腿 · Chinese ham

魷魚 · soaked squid

七星轉盤 · Seven-Star Combination Plate

五色拼盤 · Five-Appetizer Plate

三色素拼盤 · Three-Appetizer Combination Plate

雙色拼盤 · Two-Appetizer Disk

五味魷魚
Epicurean Squid Platter

發泡魷魚 300公克

1	水 10杯	**2**	番茄醬 1¹/₃大匙
	蔥 5段		醬油膏 1大匙
	薑 2片		蔥末 2小匙
	酒 1大匙		蒜末、薑末、細砂糖
			.... 各1¹/₂小匙
			紅辣椒末、麻油各1小匙
			黑醋、白醋 . 各³/₄小匙
			味精 .... ¹/₈小匙

1 魷魚去皮洗淨，內面切花刀，再切成３×５公分寬片狀。
2 **1**料煮開，入魷魚川燙至捲起時即撈起，以冷開水漂涼，瀝乾置盤中。
3 **2**料拌勻，即為沾料。

■ 發泡魷魚：魷魚洗淨，泡溫水３小時，撈出後，再放入鹼水中泡６小時，取出，續入清水內泡６小時，泡時需常換水以去鹼味，待漲發後即可使用。

²/₃ lb. (300 g) soaked squid

1 ⎡ 10 C. water
⎢ 5 sections green onion (1¹/₄")
⎢ 2 slices ginger root
⎣ 1 T. cooking wine

2 ⎡ 1¹/₃ T. ketchup
⎢ 1 T. thick soy sauce
⎢ 2 t. minced green onion
⎢ 1¹/₂ t. each: minced garlic cloves,
⎢   minced ginger root, sugar
⎢ 1 t. each: minced red chili pepper, sesame oil
⎣ ³/₄ t. each: black vinegar, white vinegar

1 Peel off the outer membrane of the squid, diagonally score the inner surface, then cut into 3 x 5 cm (1" x 2") slices.
2 Bring **1** to boiling. Parboil the squid until the pieces curl up. Remove from the wok immediately. Rinse under cold water to cool, drain.
3 Mix **2** well to make the dipping sauce. Serve the squid with the sauce.

■ Soaked Squid: Rinse the squid and soak it in warm water for 3 hours; remove and place it in baking soda water to cover; baking soda solution may be doubled. Soak for 6 hours; change the water 3 or 4 times during the soaking to remove the baking soda. When the squid has expanded, it is ready for use.

芹菜魷魚
Dried Squid with Celery

芹菜（淨重）...... 200公克   乾魷魚 100公克
紅辣椒 1條

1 ⎡ 水 2大匙
⎢ 酒 1大匙
⎢ 醬油、太白粉 各1小匙
⎢ 鹽、糖、白醋各¹/₂小匙
⎣ 胡椒粉 .... ¹/₈小匙

1 乾魷魚洗淨，泡水３０分鐘後，順紋切５公分長細條；芹菜洗淨切段；紅辣椒洗淨去籽切絲備用。
2 鍋熱入油２大匙燒熱，入魷魚炒至捲曲，再入芹菜、紅辣椒炒勻，以**1**料調味即可。

7 oz. (200 g) celery (net weight)
3¹/₂ oz. (100 g) dried squid
1 red chili pepper

1 ⎡ 2 T. water
⎢ 1 T. cooking wine
⎢ 1 t. each: soy sauce, cornstarch
⎢ ¹/₂ t. each: salt, sugar, white vinegar
⎣ ¹/₈ t. pepper

1 Wash dried squid and soak in water for 30 minutes. Cut according to the grain into 5 cm (2") shreds. Wash celery and cut into serving sections. Wash red chili pepper, discard the seeds and shred.
2 Heat a wok. Add 2T. oil. Stir-fry shredded squid until the pieces curl up. Add celery and red chili pepper. Season with **1**, and mix well. Serve.

芥末魷魚
Squid with Wasabi Sauce

發泡魷魚 400公克

1
蔥 5段
薑 2片
酒 1大匙

2
醬油 1大匙
味噌 1/2大匙
糖 2小匙
薑泥 1小匙

3 芥末粉、溫開水各2小匙

1 魷魚去皮洗淨，內面切花刀，再切成３×５公分寬片狀。
2 水１０杯加**1**料煮開，入魷魚川燙至捲起時即撈起，漂涼瀝乾備用。
3 **2**、**3**料分別拌勻後，再混合拌勻即可。不喜歡吃芥末者，可不加**3**料，直接沾食**2**料。

■ 發泡魷魚：魷魚洗淨，泡溫水３小時，撈出後，再放入鹼水中泡６小時，取出，續入清水內泡６小時，泡時需常換水以去鹼味，待漲發後即可使用。

---

14 oz. (400 g) soaked squid

1
- 5 sections green onion (1 1/4")
- 2 slices ginger root
- 1 T. cooking wine

2
- 1 T. soy sauce
- 1/2 T. miso
- 2 t. sugar
- 1 t. ginger roots paste

3 2 t. each: wasabi powder, lukewarm water

1 Peel off the outer membrane of the squid, diagonally score the inner surface, then cut into 3 x 5 cm (1" x 2") slices.
2 Bring 10C. water and **1** to a boil. Parboil squid until the pieces of curl up. Rinse under cold water to cool, drain and pat dry.
3 Mix **2** and **3** in separate bowls, then mix well together to make the dipping sauce. Serve the squid with the sauce. For those who prefer a milder taste, sauce **2** can be served alone.

■ Soaked Squid: Rinse the squid and soak it in warm water for 3 hours; remove and place it in baking soda water to cover; baking soda solution may be doubled. Soak for 6 hours; change the water 3 or 4 times during the soaking to remove the baking soda. When the squid has expanded, it is ready for use.

香酥花枝
Deep-Fried Calamari

花枝（淨重）...... 400公克　　地瓜粉 1杯

1
蛋白 1個
太白粉、玉米粉 各1大匙
酒 2小匙
五香粉 .... 1/2 小匙
鹽、味精 ..... 各1/4 小匙

1 花枝洗淨切６×１公分長條，入**1**料醃２０分鐘備用。
2 鍋熱入油３杯燒至八分熱（約１８０℃），將花枝沾地瓜粉入鍋炸至金黃色後，撈出瀝油即可。

14 oz. (400 g) cuttlefish (net weight)
1 C. cornstarch

1
- 1 egg white
- 2 T. cornstarch
- 2 t. cooking wine
- 1/2 t. five-spice powder
- 1/4 t. salt

1 Wash cuttlefish and cut into 6 x 1 cm (2 1/2"x 1/2") long strips. Marinate with **1** for 20 minutes.
2 Heat a wok. Add 3C. oil and heat to 180°C (350°F). Coat the cuttlefish strips with cornstarch and deep-fry until golden. Remove and drain. Serve.

炒蟹腳
Basil Flavored Crab Claws

蟹腳 250公克		九層塔 40公克	

1 蒜末、薑末 各1小匙

2 ⎰ 酒、醬油 各1大匙
⎱ 糖 .... ³/₄小匙

1 蟹腳洗淨以刀面略拍；九層塔洗淨去梗備用。
2 鍋熱入油3杯燒至八分熱（約180℃），入蟹腳炸至熟後（約3分鐘），撈起瀝油。
3 鍋內留油2小匙，入**1**料爆香，續入蟹腳及**2**料拌炒數下，最後入九層塔拌勻即可。

8³/₄ oz. (250 g) crab claws
1¹/₃ oz. (40 g) fresh basil

1 1 t. each: minced garlic cloves,
minced ginger roots

2 ⎰ 1 T. each: cooking wine, soy sauce
⎱ ³/₄ t. sugar

1 Wash crab claws, and crack the shell with a mallet. Wash fresh basil and discard the stems.
2 Heat a wok . Add 3 C. oil and heat to 180 °C (350 °F). Deep-fry the crab claws until cooked (about 3 minutes). Remove from the oil and drain.
3 Reserve 2t. oil in the wok. Stir-fry **1** until fragrant. Add crab claws and **2** , stir-fry and mix well. Stir in basil leaves and serve.

薑汁花枝
Ginger Flavored Cuttlefish

花枝（淨重）...... 300公克		小黃瓜 150公克	
鹽 .... ¹/₄小匙			

1 ⎡ 淡醬油、白醋、嫩薑末
.... 各1大匙
⎢ 麻油 .... ¹/₂大匙
⎢ 糖 .... ¹/₂小匙
⎣ 鹽 .... ¹/₄小匙

1 花枝洗淨切花刀，再切成6×4公分之斜薄片。
2 水6杯燒開，將花枝片入鍋川燙，見肉色轉白時即可撈出漂涼瀝乾。
3 小黃瓜切斜薄片，加鹽醃10分鐘後，以冷開水漂洗瀝乾，排盤，再將燙好的花枝片整齊鋪蓋於上，最後淋上**1**料即可。

---

²/₃ lb. (300 g net weight) cuttlefish
¹/₃ lb. (150 g) gherkin cucumbers
¹/₄ t. salt

1 ⎡ 1 T. each: thin soy sauce, white vinegar,
minced ginger roots
⎢ ¹/₂ T. sesame oil
⎢ ¹/₂ t. sugar
⎣ ¹/₄ t. salt

1 Wash cuttlefish. Cut diagonal slits over the surface and then cut into 6x4cm (2¹/₂"x1¹/₂") diagonal pieces.
2 Bring 6C. water to a boil. Parboil the cuttlefish then remove from the water as soon as the cuttlefish turns white. Rinse under cold water and drain.
3 Slice cucumber thinly. Marinate with salt for 10 minutes, rinse with water, drain and place on a plate. Arrange cuttlefish neatly over cucumber. Pour **1** over the top and serve.

涼拌花枝
Cold Cuttlefish Platter

花枝（淨重）...... 300公克　　西芹 150公克
紅辣椒絲 10公克

1
薑 2片
酒 1大匙

2
醬油 1¹/₂大匙
蒜末、麻油 各1大匙
糖、白醋 各1小匙
黑醋 .... ¹/₈小匙

1　花枝洗淨切條狀；西芹洗淨去老纖維亦切條狀備用。
2　水6杯煮開，先入西芹燙熟，取出以冰開水漂涼後，瀝乾置盤，再入**1**料及花枝燙熟，取出以冰開水漂涼，瀝乾水分後，置西芹上。
3　**2**料拌勻，淋在花枝上，最後灑上紅辣椒絲即可。

■西芹可以蘆筍取代。

$^2/_3$ **lb. (300 g) cuttlefish (net weight)**
$^1/_3$ **lb. (150 g) celery**
$^1/_3$ **oz. (10 g) shredded red chili pepper**

1
2 slices ginger root
1 T. cooking wine

2
1¹/₂ T. soy sauce
1 T. each: minced garlic cloves, sesame oil
1 t. each: sugar, white vinegar
¹/₈ t. black vinegar

1　Wash cuttlefish and cut into serving strips. Wash celery, remove the tough strings and cut into serving strips.
2　Bring 6C. water to a boil, scald celery, remove and rinse under cold water until cool, pat dry and arrange on a platter. Add **1** to the boiling water and boil cuttlefish until done. Remove and rinse under cold water until cooled, drain and arrange over the celery.
3　Mix **2** well, pour over the cuttlefish. Sprinkle shredded red chili pepper on the top. Serve.

沙茶螃蟹
Sa-Tsa Crab

青蟹 .... 400公克　　洋蔥 50公克
紅辣椒 .... 1條　　麵粉 3大匙

1
酒、沙茶醬 各1大匙
糖 1¹/₂小匙
醬油 1小匙

1　青蟹去除鰓和內臟，洗淨，切下蟹螯以刀面略拍，蟹身分切成4－6塊，沾上麵粉；洋蔥切大片，紅辣椒亦去籽切片備用。
2　鍋熱入油3杯燒至八分熱（約180℃），入蟹塊炸至熟後（約3分鐘），撈起瀝油。
3　鍋內留油2小匙，入洋蔥炒香，續入蟹、紅辣椒及**1**料拌勻即可。

---

14 oz. (400 g) crab
1²/₃ oz. (50 g) onion
1 red chili pepper
3 T. flour

1
1 T. each: cooking wine, Barbecue(Sa Tsa)sauce
1¹/₂ t. sugar
1 t. soy sauce

1　Discard the gills of the crab and rinse. Snip off the claws and crack them carefully. Cut each crab body into four to six serving pieces and coat them with flour. Cut onion into large slices. Discard the seeds in the red chili pepper and slice.
2　Heat a wok . Add 3C. oil and heat to 180 °C (350 °F). Fry the crab until cooked (about 3 minutes). Remove and drain.
3　Reserve 2t. oil in the wok. Stir-fry onion until fragrant, add the crab, red chili pepper and **1** . Stir-fry and mix well. Serve.

嗆蜇皮
 Jellyfish in Wasabi Sauce

海蜇皮 .... 180公克　西芹 80公克

1
- 蒜末、麻油 各1大匙
- 白醋 1¹/₂大匙
- 糖 1¹/₂小匙
- 鹽 .... ³/₄小匙

2
- 芥末粉、溫開水
- 各1大匙

1 海蜇皮洗淨切細絲，泡水至軟後（約2小時），撈起，
　再用60℃溫開水10杯直接沖燙，瀝乾置盤備用。
2 西芹洗淨去老纖維後，切3公分長條狀，入開水中川
　燙，撈起漂涼瀝乾，置海蜇皮上，再入**1**料拌勻。
3 **2**料拌勻，再拌入海蜇皮內即可。

6¹/₃ oz. (180 g) jellyfish
2²/₃ oz. (80 g) celery

1
- 1 T. each: minced garlic cloves, sesame oil
- ¹/₂ T. white vinegar
- 1¹/₂ t. sugar
- ³/₄ t. salt

2 1 T. each: wasabi powder, lukewarm water

1 Wash jellyfish and shred thinly. Soak in water
  until soft (about 2 hours), remove. Scald shredded jellyfish in 10C. warm water (60 °C 140 °F).
  Remove from the water and drain. Arrange on a
  plate.
2 Wash celery, remove tough strings, and cut into
  3 cm (1") sections. Blanch in boiling water and
  rinse under cold water to cool. Place on top of
  the jellyfish. Mix **1** in well.
3 Pour **2** mixture over jellyfish and celery. Mix well
  and serve.

蜇皮拌蘿蔔絲
Jellyfish with Turnips

白蘿蔔絲 .... 300公克　海蜇皮 150公克
蔥末、麻油 .... 各1大匙　鹽 .... ¹/₂小匙

1
- 醬油 2大匙
- 麻油 1大匙
- 糖 2小匙
- 白醋 1小匙

1 海蜇皮洗淨切細絲，泡水至軟後（約2小時），撈起，
　再用60℃溫開水10杯直接沖燙，瀝乾備用。
2 白蘿蔔絲加鹽醃15分鐘後擠乾水份，上置蔥末；另麻
　油燒熱，淋在蔥末與蘿蔔絲上，再入海蜇皮、**1**料拌勻
　即可。

---

²/₃ lb. (300 g) shredded turnip
¹/₃ lb. (150 g) jellyfish
1 T. each: minced green onion, sesame oil
¹/₂ t. salt

1
- 2 T. soy sauce
- 1 T. sesame oil
- 2 t. sugar
- 1 t. white vinegar

1 Wash jellyfish and shred thinly. Soak in water
  until soft (about 2 hours), remove. Scald the
  shredded jellyfish in 10C. warm water (60°C
  140°F). Remove from the water and drain.
2 Marinate the turnip with salt for 15 minutes,
  squeeze out the liquid, then arrange on a plate.
  Sprinkle green onion over the turnip, then pour
  the heated sesame oil over the top. Mix in the
  jelly fish and **1** thoroughly. Serve.

糖醋蜇皮
Sweet and Sour Jellyfish

海蜇皮	.... 200公克	小黃瓜	.... 140公克
胡蘿蔔	.... 80克	薑	.... 25克
紅辣椒	...............2¹/₂條		

┏ 白醋 5大匙
┃ 糖 4大匙
┃ 蒜末 1¹/₂大匙
１┃ 麻油 1大匙
┃ 醬油 1小匙
┃ 鹽 .... ¹/₄小匙
┗ 味精 .... ¹/₈小匙

1 海蜇皮洗淨切細絲，泡水至軟後（約2小時），撈起，
　再用60℃溫開水10杯直接沖燙，瀝乾備用。
2 小黃瓜、薑洗淨切絲，胡蘿蔔去皮洗淨切絲，紅辣椒洗
　淨，剖開去籽亦切絲備用。
3 所有材料及１料混合拌勻，蓋上保鮮膜，冷藏醃泡4至
　6小時即可。

7 oz. (200 g) jellyfish
5¹/₄ oz. (140 g) gherkin cucumbers
2²/₃ oz. (80 g) carrot
1 oz. (25 g) ginger roots
2¹/₂ red chili peppers

┏ **5 T. white vinegar**
┃ **4 T. sugar**
┃ **1¹/₂ T. minced garlic cloves**
１┃ **1 T. sesame oil**
┃ **1 t. soy sauce**
┗ **¹/₄ t. salt**

1 Wash jellyfish and shred thinly. Soak in water
　until soft (about 2 hours), remove. Scald the shred-
　ded jelly fish in 10C. warm water (60°C 140°F).
　Remove from the water and drain.
2 Wash cucumbers and ginger roots, shred both.
　Peel the carrot, wash and shred. Wash red chili
　peppers, discard the seeds and shred.
3 Mix all the ingredients and **１** well . Cover with
　plastic wrap, refrigerate 4 to 6 hours. Serve.

銀魚花生
Silver Fish and Peanuts

銀魚	.... 200公克	蒜頭花生	.... 80公克
紅辣椒片、蔥末	.. 各2大匙	蒜末	.... 1 大匙

┏ 酒 .... 1 大匙
┃ 糖 .... ¹/₂小匙
１┃ 鹽 .... ¹/₄小匙
┗ 胡椒粉 .... 少許

1 銀魚洗淨，瀝乾備用（若太鹹，則略泡水）。
2 鍋熱入油4杯燒至八分熱（約180℃），入銀魚炸至
　金黃色後，撈起瀝油備用。
3 鍋內留油2大匙燒熱，入辣椒片、蔥末、蒜末爆香，再
　入銀魚、花生及１料拌勻即可。

7 oz. (200 g) silver fish
2²/₃ oz. (80 g) garlic flavored peanuts
2 T. each: red chili pepper slices,
**　　　minced green onion**
1 T. minced garlic cloves

┏ **1 T. cooking wine**
┃ **¹/₂ t. sugar**
１┃ **¹/₄ t. salt**
┗ **dash pepper**

1 Wash silver fish, drain. If the fish is too salty,
　soak in water for a while.
2 Heat a wok . Add 4C. oil and heat to 180°C
　(350 °F). Deep-fry silver fish until golden, remove
　from oil and drain.
3 Reserve 2T. oil in the wok. Stir-fry red chili pep-
　per, minced green onion, and minced garlic
　cloves until fragrant. Add silver fish, peanuts and
　１ . Mix well and serve.

燻魚
Soo Chow Fish

草魚（中段）...... 600公克　八角 10顆

1 醬油 .... 2²/₃ 大匙　　**2** 水 1杯
　　紹興酒 .... 1大匙　　　　糖 4大匙

1　草魚洗淨切1公分厚片，入**1**料拌醃2小時以上（每隔
　　1小時翻面一次，使之調味均勻）；**2**料加熱煮溶為糖
　　水。
2　鍋熱入油3杯燒至七分熟（約160℃），入一半魚片
　　以小火炸至酥脆後（約15分鐘），撈起，趁熱入糖水
　　內浸泡。油鍋續入另一半魚片炸酥，再把泡過糖水之魚
　　片撈起，入另一半魚片泡糖水約10分鐘。
3　另鍋熱入油2大匙燒熱，入八角炒香，再入魚片及剩餘
　　之**1**、**2**料，改小火加蓋燜煮約3分鐘後，打開鍋蓋，
　　續入2大匙油，至汁快收乾只剩油即可。

■本道菜可熱食亦可冷食，但冷食風味更佳。

1¹/₃ lb. (600 g) grass fish (middle section only)
10 star anises

1 2²/₃ T. soy sauce
1 T. Chinese Shao-Shin wine

2 1 C. water
4 T. sugar

1　Wash grass fish, cut into 1 cm (¹/₂") thick slices.
Marinate in **1** for 2 hours (turn every hour to even
the flavor). Bring **2** to a boil to make syrup.
2　Heat a wok to 160°C (320°F), add 3C. oil. Deep-
fry half of the fish slices over low heat until crispy
(about 15 minutes). Remove from oil and soak in
syrup for about 10 minutes. Repeat with the remaining half of the fish slices.
3　Heat a clean wok, add 2T. oil. Stir-fry star anises
until fragrant, add fish slices and the remaining **1**
and **2** . Cover with lid and simmer over low heat
for 3 minutes. Remove the lid, add 2T. oil, and
simmer until the sauce dries out (only oil should
remain on the bottom of the wok). Serve.

■ This dish can be served warm or cold. Serving
cold may improve the taste.

酥炸生蠔
Oyster Fritters

生蠔 250公克

1 太白粉 .... 1大匙　　　**2** 低筋麵粉 .... ³/₄杯
　　鹽 .... ¹/₂小匙　　　　　冰水 5大匙
　　　　　　　　　　　　　　　　　　　　油 3大匙
　　　　　　　　　　　　　　　　　　　　蛋黃 1個
　　　　　　　　　　　　　　　　　　　　鹽 .... ³/₈小匙
　　　　　　　　　　　　　　　　　　　　味精 .... ¹/₈小匙

1　生蠔加**1**料抓洗，再用水沖洗乾淨，瀝乾，續以乾布將
　　表面水份完全吸乾。**2**料輕輕拌勻後（避免出筋），入
　　生蠔稍拌勻備用。
2　鍋熱入油4杯燒至八分熱（約180℃），以湯匙舀生
　　蠔入鍋炸至金黃色，撈起瀝油，食時可沾椒鹽或番茄
　　醬。

8²/₃ oz. (250 g) oysters

1 1 T. cornstarch
¹/₂ t. salt

2 ³/₄ C. low gluten flour
5 T. ice water
3 T. oil
1 egg yolk
³/₈ t. salt

1　Mix oysters in **1** , rub gently with fingers. Rinse
with water, drain. Pat dry with kitchen towel. Mix
2 gently, add oysters to the batter and stir slightly.
2　Heat a wok. Add 4C. oil and heat to 180°C
(350 °F). Spoon oyster batter into the hot oil and
fry until golden. Remove from the oil and drain.
May be served with pepper salt or ketchup.

炸烏魚子
Deep-Fried Fish Roe (Karasumi)

烏魚子（1付）.. 100公克	花枝 100公克
紫菜 1張	白蘿蔔（淨重）.... 60公克
蒜白 ....（淨重）30公克	酒 2大匙

1
- 太白粉 1大匙
- 鹽 1/4小匙
- 味精 1/8小匙

1　將烏魚子切成兩半，入酒醃泡至軟後，撕去表面薄膜；花枝剁碎，入**1**料拌醃即為花枝漿；紫菜切成2張，分別將烏魚子包起來，外層再裹上花枝漿備用。

2　鍋熱入油6杯燒至六分熱（約140℃），入烏魚子炸至浮出油面後即撈起，瀝乾油份，待涼切斜薄片。

3　白蘿蔔切斜薄片，蒜白亦切斜片，分別平鋪於盤底，再鋪上烏魚子，食時可依個人喜好配食白蘿蔔或蒜白。

3$^1/_2$ oz.(100 g) (one whole) fish roe
1 sheet dried seaweed
3$^1/_2$ oz.(100 g) cuttlefish
2 oz.(60 g) turnip
1 oz.(30 g) fresh garlic (white part only net weight)
2 T. cooking wine

1
- **1 T. cornstarch**
- **$^1/_4$ t. salt**

1　Separate the fish roe into two parts. Marinate in cooking wine until soft. Peel off the surface membrane. Chop cuttlefish finely and mix well with **1** to make a cuttlefish paste. Snip seaweed sheet into two pieces and wrap up the fish roe. Coat with cuttlefish paste.

2　Heat a wok. Add 6C. oil and heat to 140 °C (280°F). Deep-fry the seaweed-wrapped fish roe until they float. Remove from the oil and drain. When cool, cut into thin diagonal slices.

3　Slice turnip into thin pieces. Cut fresh garlic into thin diagonal slices. Spread both at the bottom of a plate. Arrange fish roe slices on top. Fish roe slices may be eaten with either turnip or fresh garlic or both, depending upon personal preference.

梅汁泡河蜆
Clams in Plum Sauce

河蜆 300公克	話梅 6粒

1
- 蒜頭 5粒
- 薑 2片
- 紅辣椒 1條
- 醬油膏 1/4杯
- 醬油 1大匙
- 味精 1/8小匙

1　河蜆加水蓋過其身，使之吐砂（約4小時），撈起洗淨，再加水蓋過其身，入水中以隔水加熱方法煮至河蜆略開口，待湯汁稍白濁時即可撈出，瀝乾水份備用。

2　話梅以溫開水1/2杯泡約15分鐘後，撈出話梅，餘汁留用；蒜頭洗淨去皮拍碎，辣椒洗淨切斜片備用。

3　將河蜆、梅汁及**1**料拌勻，蓋上保鮮膜，冷藏醃泡6小時即可。

$^2/_3$ lb. (300 g) fresh water clams
6 preserved sour plums

1
- **5 garlic cloves**
- **2 slices ginger root**
- **1 red chili pepper**
- **$^1/_4$ C. thick soy sauce**
- **1 T. soy sauce**

1　Soak the clams in water to rid them of sand (about 4 hours). Drain and rinse. Cover the clams with water, place in hot water bath over a double boiler. Heat until the clams open up slightly and the water becomes a little turbid. Remove and drain.

2　Soak the plums in $^1/_2$ C. lukewarm water for about 15 minutes. Discard the plums. Wash the garlic cloves, peel off the skins and crush with the back of a knife. Wash red chili pepper and slice.

3　Mix the clams, plum juice, and **1** together and cover with plastic wrap. Refrigerate for 6 hours and serve.

香煎鯧魚
Browned Pomfret

白鯧魚 300公克

1	番茄 70公克	**2**	醬油 3大匙
	洋蔥 50公克		酒、蔥末 各2大匙
	芹菜 20公克		糖 1大匙
	紅辣椒 1條		鹽 1/8小匙
	薑 2片		

1 鯧魚去內臟及頭尾，洗淨，剖開魚身剔除大骨後，魚肉備用。
2 番茄、洋蔥洗淨切小丁；芹菜去葉洗淨切末；紅辣椒洗淨去籽切斜片；薑切絲備用。
3 魚肉入 **1**、**2** 料拌勻，醃約３０分鐘後取出。
4 鍋熱入油２大匙燒熱，入魚肉兩面煎至金黃色即可。

---

²/₃ lb. (300 g) white pomfret

1
- 2¹/₃ oz. (70 g) tomato
- 1²/₃ oz. (50 g) onion
- ²/₃ oz. (20 g) celery
- 1 red chili pepper
- 2 slices ginger root

2
- 3 T. soy sauce
- 2 T. each: cooking wine, minced green onion
- 1 T. sugar
- 1/8 t. salt

1 Discard the entrails and remove the head and tail of the fish, rinse. Cut fish in half lengthwise, and remove the backbone.
2 Wash and dice tomato and onion. Discard the leaves and mince the celery. Wash red chili pepper, discard the seeds and slice. Shred the ginger roots.
3 Mix **1** and **2** well. Marinate the fish in the mixture for 30 minutes. Remove.
4 Heat a wok. Add 2T. oil. Saute the fish on both sides until golden brown.

鹹蜆
Salted Clams

河蜆 300公克

1	蒜頭 5粒
	薑 2片
	紅辣椒 1條
	醬油、冷開水　各4大匙
	酒 1/2大匙
	糖、黑醋 各1小匙
	味精 1/4小匙

1 河蜆處理方法請參照梅汁泡河蜆之作法１。
2 蒜頭洗淨去皮拍碎，紅辣椒洗淨切斜片備用。
3 將河蜆及 **1** 料拌勻，蓋上保鮮膜，冷藏醃泡６小時即可。

---

²/₃ lb. (300 g) fresh water clams

1
- 5 garlic cloves
- 2 slices ginger root
- 1 red chili pepper
- 4 T. each: soy sauce, cold water
- 1/2 T. cooking wine
- 1 t. each: sugar, black vinegar

1 Prepare and cook the clams as in "Clams in Plum Sauce", page 27.
2 Wash garlic cloves, peel off the skins and crush with the back of a knife. Wash red chili pepper and slice.
3 Mix the clams and **1** together, cover with plastic wrap. Refrigerate for 6 hours and serve.

蔥烤鯽魚
Gold Carp Topped with Green Onions

鯽魚(淨重) .... 450公克　蔥 300公克

1
- 白醋 5大匙
- 冰糖、醬油 各4大匙
- 味精 1/2小匙

1　鯽魚、蔥均洗淨，蔥切10公分長段備用。
2　鍋熱入油6杯燒至八分熱（180℃），入蔥段炸至表面稍黃後，撈起備用；餘油再加熱，續入鯽魚以大火炸酥，撈出瀝油，再以**1**料醃泡3小時（浸泡時每隔半小時翻面一次，使魚均勻浸泡）。
3　取1/2炸過的蔥段墊在鍋底，上置鯽魚，再放上剩餘的蔥，並淋下醃魚所剩之汁液，加水1杯煮開，蓋上鍋蓋，改小火續煮3小時至湯汁收乾後，待涼即可供食。

---

1 lb. (450 g) gold carp
2/3 lb. (300 g) green onions

1
- **5T. white vinegar**
- **4T. each: crystal sugar, soy sauce**

1　Wash the green onions and gold carp. Cut the green onions into 10 cm (4") long sections.
2　Heat a wok. Add 6C. oil and heat to 180°C (350°F). Deep-fry the green onions until lightly browned, remove from oil and drain. Heat the remaining oil. Deep-fry the gold carp over high heat until crispy. Remove from oil and drain. Marinate the gold carp in **1** for 3 hours, turning every half hour to destribute the flavor.
3　Place 1/3 of the fried green onions at the bottom of the wok. Put the gold carp on top of the green onions, then arrange the remaining green onions on top of the gold carp. Pour the remaining marinating sauce over the top. Add 1C. water, bring to a boil, cover. Reduce to low heat and simmer for 3 hours, until sauce evaporates. Cool and serve.

芝麻蝦
Sesame Shrimp

劍蝦 .... 300公克　酒 1大匙
熟白芝麻 2小匙

1
- 水 1大匙
- 糖 2小匙
- 醬油、麥芽糖　各1小匙

1　劍蝦剪除鬚腳，去腸泥洗淨瀝乾，加酒拌醃5分鐘後瀝乾備用。
2　鍋熱入油3杯燒至八分熱（180℃），入蝦大火炸酥後（約2分鐘），撈起瀝油。
3　鍋內留油1小匙，入蝦及**1**料小火拌炒至汁液收乾，再入芝麻拌勻即可。

2/3 lb. (300 g) shrimp
1 T. cooking wine
2 t. roasted white sesame

1
- **1 T. water**
- **2 t. sugar**
- **1 t. each: soy sauce, maltose**

1　Trim off the whiskers and devein the shrimp. Wash and drain. Marinate with wine for 5 minutes and drain.
2　Heat a wok. Add 3C. oil and heat to 180°C (350°F). Deep-fry the shrimp until crispy (about 2 minutes). Remove from the oil and drain.
3　Reserve 1t. oil in the wok, add shrimp and **1**. Stir-fry until sauce reduces completely. Mix in sesame seeds and serve.

五香酥蝦
Five-Spice Crispy Shrimp

劍蝦	300公克	蔥	15公克
紅辣椒	1條	酒	2小匙
薑末	1/2小匙		

1
- 酒 1小匙
- 五香粉 1/2小匙
- 鹽 3/8小匙
- 胡椒粉 1/2小匙

1 劍蝦剪除鬚腳、去腸泥，洗淨瀝乾，加酒拌醃１０分鐘後瀝乾；蔥洗淨切末，紅辣椒洗淨去籽切末備用。
2 鍋熱入油３杯燒至八分熱（約１８０℃），入蝦炸酥後（約２分鐘），撈起瀝油。
3 鍋內留油１小匙燒熱，入蔥末、薑末、紅辣椒末炒香，再入炸好之蝦及 **1** 料拌勻即可。

2/3 lb. (300 g) shrimp
1/2 oz. (15 g) green onions
1 red chili pepper
2 t. cooking wine
1/2 t. minced ginger roots

1
- **1 t. cooking wine**
- **1/2 t. five-spice powder**
- **3/8 t. salt**
- **1/2 t. pepper**

1 Trim off the whiskers and devein the shrimp without removing the shell, rinse and drain. Marinate with wine for 10 minutes, drain. Wash green onions and mince. Wash red chili pepper, discard the seeds and mince.
2 Heat a wok. Add 3C. oil and heat to 180°C (350°F). Fry the shrimp until crispy (about 2 minutes). Remove from the oil and drain.
3 Reserve 1t. oil in the wok. Stir-fry minced green onion, minced ginger roots, and minced red chili pepper until fragrant. Add fried shrimp, season with **1**, and mix well. Serve.

鹽酥蝦
Crispy Garlic Shrimp

劍蝦	300公克	酒	1大匙

1
- 蒜末 2大匙
- 紅辣椒末 1小匙

2
- 鹽 1/3小匙
- 味精 3/8小匙

1 劍蝦剪除鬚腳，去腸泥洗淨瀝乾，加酒拌勻醃５分鐘後，瀝乾備用。
2 鍋熱入油３杯燒至八分熱（約１８０℃），入蝦炸酥後（約２分鐘），撈起瀝油。
3 鍋內留油１小匙，入 **1** 料炒香，再入炸好之蝦及 **2** 料拌勻即可。

■ 劍蝦可以紅蝦、河蝦或鱸蝦取代。

2/3 lb. (300 g) shrimp
1 T. cooking wine

1
- **2 T. minced garlic cloves**
- **1 t. minced red chili pepper**

2 **2/3 t. salt**

1 Trim off the whiskers and devein the shrimp without removing the shell, wash and drain. Marinate with wine for 5 minutes and drain.
2 Heat a wok. Add 3C. oil and heat to 180°C (350 °F). Deep-fry the shrimp until crispy (about 2 minutes). Remove from oil and drain.
3 Reserve 1t. oil in the wok. Stir-fry **1** until fragrant. Mix in fried shrimp and season with **2**. Mix well and serve.

■ Any type of shrimp may be used for this recipe.

腐皮香捲
Tofu Skin Rolls

豆包（3塊）....... 130公克　九層塔（淨重）.... 75公克
豆皮 2張

1[蛋 .... 1個　**2** 麵粉、水 各1小匙
糖、麻油 各1小匙
鹽 1/2小匙
味精 1/8小匙

1　豆包洗淨切小丁，九層塔洗淨切末，二者加**1**料拌勻即
　　為內餡，分成8等份備用。
2　每張豆皮切成4小張，每張豆皮上各置1份內餡，包成
　　春捲狀，接口處以**2**料黏緊。
3　鍋熱入油4杯燒至七分熱（約160℃），入豆腐皮捲
　　炸至金黃色後（約2分鐘），撈出瀝油即可。

■九層塔可以香菜取代。

4¹/₂ oz. (130 g) bean curd pouch (3 pieces)
2¹/₂ oz. (75 g) fresh basil leaves
2 dried bean curd skins

1[1 egg
1 t. each: sugar, sesame oil
1/2 t. salt

2 1 t. each: flour, water

1　Wash bean curd pouch and dice. Wash basil and
　　mince. Mix both with **1** to make the filling. Sep-
　　arate into 8 equal portions.
2　Cut each bean curd skin into 4 equal pieces. Place
　　a portion of filling in the middle and roll it up as
　　a spring roll. Seal the openings with **2**.
3　Heat a wok. Add 4C. oil and heat to 160°C
　　(320 °F). Fry the rolls until golden (about 2 min-
　　utes). Remove and drain. Serve.

■ Basil may be replaced by coriander.

菠菜拌皮蛋
Spinach Salad with Preserved Eggs

菠菜 .... 300公克　小豆干 120公克
中式火腿 .... 40公克　皮蛋 2個

1[麻油 1¹/₃大匙
鹽 1/2小匙
味精 1/4小匙

1　菠菜洗淨，入開水中燙熟，撈起漂涼，擠乾水份後切細
　　小丁。
2　豆干入開水中川燙，取出切細小丁，皮蛋去殼亦切細小
　　丁，中式火腿先蒸熟，再切細小丁備用。
3　將所有材料加**1**料拌勻即可。

---

²/₃ lb. (300 g) spinach
4¹/₄ oz. (120 g) small pressed bean curds
1¹/₃ oz. (40 g) Chinese ham
2 preserved eggs

1[1¹/₃ T. sesame oil
1/2 t. salt

1　Wash spinach and place in boiling water. Sim-
　　mer 2 minutes. Rinse under cold water to cool,
　　squeeze off the water and chop.
2　Blanch pressed bean curds in boiling water, re-
　　move and dice. Peel off the shells and dice the
　　preserved eggs. Steam Chinese ham and dice.
3　Mix all the ingredients well and season with **1**.
　　Serve.

炸豆腐
Deep-Fried Tofu

豆腐 2塊

1
┌ 醬油 2大匙
│ 香菜末、蔥末 ....
│ 各1⅓大匙
│ 蒜末、辣椒末、糖、黑
│ 醋 各1½小匙
└ 味精、胡椒粉各¼小匙

1. 豆腐每塊切成１０小方塊；**1**料拌勻備用。
2. 鍋熱入油６杯燒至八分熱（１８０℃），入豆腐炸至金黃色後撈起，瀝油排盤，食時沾**1**料即可。

---

2 tofu (bean curd)

1
┌ 2 T. soy sauce
│ 1⅓ T. each: minced coriander,
│ minced green onion
│ 1½ t. each: minced garlic cloves,
│ minced red chili pepper, sugar,
│ black vinegar
└ ¼ t. pepper

1. Cut each tofu into 10 small squares. Mix **1** well to make the dipping sauce.
2. Heat a wok. Add 6C. oil and heat to 180°C (350 °F). Deep-fry tofu until golden. Remove from the oil and drain. Serve with **1** sauce.

青椒拌皮蛋・ *Green Pepper and Preserved Eggs*

青椒拌皮蛋
Green Pepper and Preserved Eggs

青椒 .... 300公克　皮蛋 2個

1
┌ 麻油 2小匙
│ 胡椒粉 .... ¾小匙
└ 鹽、味精 ...... 各½小匙

1. 青椒洗淨去籽，入烤箱以２５０℃烤１０分鐘，取出待涼切成小細丁。
2. 皮蛋去殼切碎，入青椒及**1**料拌勻即可。

⅔ lb. (300 g) green bell pepper
2 preserved eggs

1
┌ 2 t. sesame oil
│ ¾ t. pepper
└ ½ t. salt

1. Wash green bell pepper and discard the seeds. Heat oven to 250°C (480°F) and roast for 10 minutes. Remove from oven and leave to cool. Dice finely.
2. Peel off the shells and mince the eggs. Mix well with green bell pepper. Add **1** and serve.

炸豆腐・ *Deep-Fried Tofu*

漲蛋
Egg Cake

蛋 .... 4個　　油條 2條
絞肉 .... 30公克　　蔥 4枝
蝦米 1大匙

1┌油 2小匙
　├鹽 1/2小匙
　└味精 1/4小匙

1　蝦米洗淨切末，蔥2枝洗淨切末，另2枝切長段，油條
　　泡水至軟後，擠乾水份切末。
2　蛋打散，加蝦米、絞肉、蔥末、油條及**1**料拌勻。
3　鍋熱入油6大匙燒熱，入蔥段爆香至金黃色，續入蛋液
　　（不要攪拌）並加蓋，隨即改微小火烘30分鐘後，取
　　出切片，焦面朝上即可。

4 eggs
2 Chinese crullers
1 oz. (30 g) ground pork
4 stalks green onion
1 T. dried baby shrimp

1┌**2 t. oil**
　└**1/2 t. salt**

1　Wash dried shrimp and mince. Mince 2 stalks of
　　the green onion, and section the other 2 stalks.
　　Soak the crullers in water until soft, squeeze off
　　water and mince.
2　Beat the eggs, mix in shrimp, ground pork,
　　minced green onion , minced crullers and **1** .
3　Heat wok and add 6T. oil. Stir-fry the green on-
　　ion sections until golden brown. Pour in the egg
　　mixture (do not stir). Cover with a lid, turn the
　　heat to low and pot roast for 30 minutes. Remove
　　and slice. Arrange the slices, fried side up, on a
　　plate. Serve.

漲蛋・Egg Cake

三色蛋 ・ Tricolored Egg Cold Cuts

三色蛋
Tricolored Egg Cold Cuts

蛋 .... 3個　　生鹹蛋、皮蛋 各2個

1┌水 5大匙
　├酒、醬油 各1小匙
　└胡椒粉 .... 少許

1　鹹蛋煮熟後，與皮蛋均去殼切丁備用。
2　蛋打散，入皮蛋、鹹蛋及**1**料拌勻後，入鍋蒸10分鐘
　　至蛋液凝固，取出待涼切片即可。

3 eggs
2 each: raw salty eggs, preserved eggs

1┌**5 T. water**
　├**1 t. each: cooking wine, soy sauce**
　└**dash pepper**

1　Boil the salty eggs until cooked. Peel the shells
　　off the salty eggs and the preserved eggs, dice
　　both.
2　Beat the eggs, mix with salty eggs, preserved eggs
　　and **1** . Steam for 10 minutes or until firmly set.
　　Remove and cool. Slice and serve.

雞捲
Chicken Rolls

絞肉、魚漿、洋蔥 ....
.... 各150公克
胡蘿蔔 30公克

洋地瓜 80公克
乾腐皮 1¹/₂張

1
太白粉 3¹/₂大匙
糖 2小匙
油蔥酥、酒、薑汁、醬
油、麻油 各1小匙
鹽 .... ³/₈小匙
味精、胡椒粉、黑胡椒
粉、五香粉 .. 各¹/₄小匙

2 麵粉、水 各2大匙

1 洋蔥、洋地瓜、胡蘿蔔分別去皮洗淨切末。
2 絞肉、魚漿、洋蔥、洋地瓜、胡蘿蔔及**1**料混合均勻即
  為內餡，分成3等份備用。
3 一張豆皮對切成2小張，每張豆皮上各置1份餡，捲成
  長條圓筒狀，接口處以調勻之**2**料黏緊。
4 鍋熱入油5杯燒至五分熱（約120℃），入雞捲小火
  炸至金黃色後（約5分鐘），撈起瀝油，切0．5公分
  厚之斜片，食時可沾番茄醬或海山醬。

■ 洋地瓜可以荸薺取代。

¹/₃ lb. (150 g) each: ground pork, fish paste,
                     onions
2³/₄ oz. (80 g) jicama
1 oz. (30 g) carrot
1¹/₂ sheets dried bean curd skin

1
3¹/₂ T. cornstarch
2 t. sugar
1 t. each: fried shallots , cooking wine,
           ginger root juice , soy sauce,
           sesame oil
³/₈ t. salt
¹/₄ t. each: pepper, black pepper powder,
            five spice powder

2 2 T. each: flour, water

1 Peel the skins off onion, jicama, and carrot. Wash
  and mince all.
2 Mix ground pork, fish paste, onion, jicama, carrot, and **1** well to make the filling. Divide the
  filling into 3 equal portions.
3 Cut one sheet bean curd skin in half. Place one
  portion of filling in the middle and roll into a cylinder, seal the openings with mixture **2** . Makes
  three rolls.
4 Heat a wok. Add 5C. oil and heat to 120°C
  (250°F). Fry the rolls over low heat until golden
  (about 5 minutes). Remove and drain, cut into
  0.5cm (¹/₄") thick slices. Serve with ketchup or
  Hoisin sauce.

■ Jicama may be replaced by water chestnuts.

雪裡紅炒蛋
Stir-Fried Eggs with Greens

蛋 4個

雪裡紅 120公克

1 鹽、味精 ...... 各¹/₄小匙

1 雪裡紅洗淨，擠乾水份後切細末，蛋打散加**1**料拌勻。
2 鍋熱入油5大匙燒熱，入雪裡紅炒熟，再倒入蛋液炒至
  凝固即可。

4 eggs
4¹/₄ oz. (120 g) salted mustard greens
¹/₄ t. salt

1 Wash salted mustard greens, squeeze off the water and mince. Beat the eggs and season with salt.
2 Heat a wok. Add 5T. oil and stir-fry minced salt
  mustard greens until tender. Pour in the eggs and
  stir-fry until the eggs are set. Serve.

紫菜蛋捲
Egg and Seaweed Rolls

里肌肉 .... 150公克　生鹹蛋黃 4個
紫菜 .... 2張　生菜 2片
酒 1小匙

1
太白粉 .... ½大匙　　**2** 麵粉、水 各1½大匙
酒 1小匙
糖 .... ½小匙
鹽、味精、胡椒粉 ......
.... 各⅛小匙

1　里肌肉切薄片，用刀背略拍，入**1**料醃１０分鐘後，分成２等份；生鹹蛋黃沾酒，入鍋蒸５分鐘，待涼壓成泥，並搓成３５公分之長條狀，再切成２段；**2**料調勻成麵糊備用。
2　取一張紫菜，上置一份肉片鋪平，抹上少許麵糊後，再鋪上一層生菜，並取一段蛋黃置紫菜之一邊，壓緊包捲成長條狀，封口處以麵糊黏住，共做成２份。
3　鍋熱入油４杯燒至八分熱（１８０℃），入紫菜捲以中火炸至肉熟後（約５分鐘），撈出，切 0.5 公分斜片即可。

---

¹/₃ lb. (150 g) pork loin
4 raw salty egg yolks
2 sheets dried seaweed (nori)
2 leaves lettuce
1 t. cooking wine

1
½ T. cornstarch
1 t. cooking wine
½ t. sugar
⅛ t. each: salt, pepper

2 1½ T. each: flour, water

1　Slice pork loin thinly. Pound until tender with a meat mallet. Marinate in **1** for 10 minutes and separate into 2 equal portions. Sprinkle wine on the yolks and steam for 5 minutes; leave to cool and crush to paste. Roll the egg paste into a 35 cm (14") long strip, then cut in half. Mix **2** into a flour paste.
2　Spread out a sheet of seaweed, lay a portion of pork evenly on the seaweed, brush with flour paste. Put a layer of lettuce and an egg strip on one side of the lettuce, then roll it tightly up as a cylinder. Seal the openings with the flour paste. Makes 2 rolls.
3　Heat a wok. Add 4C. oil and heat to 180°C (350°F). Fry the seaweed rolls over medium heat until golden (about 5 minutes). Remove from oil and drain. Cut into 0.5 cm (1/4") thick slices Serve.

五香辣豆
Spicy Soybeans

黃豆 .... 120公克　紅辣椒末、麻油 .. 各1大匙

1
八角 2顆
花椒粒 1小匙
小茴、桂皮（拍碎）..
.... 各¼小匙
沙薑 .... ⅛小匙

2
水 2½杯
辣椒醬 .... ½大匙
糖 .... 1 小匙
鹽 .... ¾小匙
味精 .... ¼小匙

1　黃豆洗淨加水浸泡５小時，撈起瀝乾；**1**料裝入滷包袋中備用。
2　鍋熱入油２大匙燒熱，入黃豆拌炒片刻，續入**2**料及滷包，小火加蓋煮至黃豆熟透（約５０分鐘），再入麻油、紅辣椒末炒至湯汁收乾即可。

4¹/₄ oz. (120 g) soybeans
1 T. each: minced red chili pepper, sesame oil

1
2 star anises
1 t. Szechwan peppercorns
¼ t. each: fennel, cinnamon (crushed)
⅛ t. sand ginger

2
2½ C. water
½ T. hot chili paste
1 t. sugar
¾ t. salt

1　Wash soybeans and soak in water for 5 hours, drain. Place **1** ingredients into a spice pouch.
2　Heat a wok, add 2T. oil. Stir-fry soybeans slightly. Add **2** and spice pouch, cover with a lid and simmer over low heat until soybeans are tender (about 50 minutes). Stir in sesame oil and minced red chili pepper. Cook uncovered until all the sauce evaporates. Serve.

素鵝
Delicious Vegetarian Rolls

乾腐皮 .... 12張　香菇 6朵

1｜榨菜絲、胡蘿蔔絲、熟
　筍絲 .... 各¹/₂杯

2｜水 2大匙
　醬油、糖、太白粉 ....
　.................... 各1小匙

3｜醬油 2小匙
　糖 .... ¹/₄小匙

1 香菇洗淨泡軟去蒂、切絲；泡香菇之水留¹/₂杯備用。
2 鍋熱入油2大匙燒熱，入香菇絲與**1**料炒勻，續入**2**料
　拌勻即為內餡，再將內餡分成3等份備用。
3 **3**料與泡香菇之水拌勻成調味汁後，將一張腐皮攤開，
　刷上調味汁，再疊上另一張腐皮，刷上調味汁，如此重
　覆疊4張後，取一份內餡置於中間，包成5×15公分
　之長條（共做3條），入蒸籠以大火蒸5分鐘，取出待
　涼。
4 鍋熱入麻油3大匙燒熱，入素鵝以小火慢煎至兩面呈金
　黃色時，取出待涼切斜厚片即可。

---

12 sheets dried bean curd skin
6 dried Chinese black mushrooms

1｜¹/₂ C. each:　shredded Szechwan pickled mus-
　　tard greens, shredded carrot ,
　　shredded boiled bamboo shoots

2｜2 T. water
　1 t. each: soy sauce, sugar, cornstarch

3｜2 t. soy sauce
　¹/₄ t. sugar

1 Wash mushrooms, soak in warm water until soft.
  Discard the stems and shred. Reserve ¹/₂ C. of the
  water for later use.
2 Heat a wok. Add 2 T. oil. Stir-fry mushrooms
  and **1**, mix well. Add **2** and mix well to make the
  filling. Separate the filling to 3 equal portions.
3 Mix **3** and water from the mushrooms to make
  the seasoning sauce. Spread out one bean curd
  skin, brush on the seasoning sauce. Layer another bean curd skin on tip, brush another film of the
  sauce. Repeat for 4 layers. Place one portion of
  filling in the center of the top sheet and roll into a
  5 x 15 cm (2"x 6") long cylinder. Repeat process
  2 more times, layering a set of 4 bean curd skins
  with seasoning sauce, adding a portion of the filling and rolling into a cylinder. Steam the rolls
  over high heat for 5 minutes, remove from steamer
  and cool.
4 Heat a wok. Add 3T. sesame oil. Saute the rolls
  over low heat until golden on both sides. Remove
  from wok and cool. Cut into thick diagonal slices and serve.

香芹干絲
Simple Delight

五香豆干 .... 200公克　芹菜 100公克
辣椒醬 2小匙

1｜醬油 2小匙
　糖、味精 ...... 各¹/₂小匙

1 豆干洗淨，每塊切成薄片，再切細絲，芹菜去頭、葉洗
　淨後，切5公分段並以刀面拍裂備用。
2 鍋熱入油3大匙燒熱，入辣椒醬炒香，再入豆干及**1**料
　以中火炒至汁液收乾後，續入水1大匙及芹菜拌炒均勻
　即可。

■ 香蔥干絲：芹菜以100公克蔥絲取代，其餘材料及做
　法同香芹干絲。

---

7 oz. (200 g) five-spice pressed bean curds
3¹/₂ oz. (100 g) Chinese celery
2 t. hot chili paste

1｜2 t. soy sauce
　¹/₄ t. sugar

1 Wash the pressed bean curds, slice them and then
  shred. Trim off the leaves and ends of the celery,
  cut into 5 cm (2") sections and shred .
2 Heat a wok, add 3T. oil. Stir-fry hot chili paste
  until fragrant. Add pressed bean curds and **1** .
  Stir-fry over medium heat until all the sauce evaporates. Add 1T. water and the celery. Stir-fry and
  mix well. Serve.

■ Green Onion and Bean Curds: Celery may be re-
　placed by 3¹/₂ oz. (100 g) of shredded green on-
　ions.
　Proceed with remaining ingredients and methods
　as directed, above.

如意豆包絲
Delightful Vegetarian Platter

黃豆芽 .... 400公克　油炸豆包 80公克
蒜苗 .... 1枝　紅辣椒 1條
薑 1片

1
水 .... 1¹/₂ 杯
醬油 2大匙
冰糖 2小匙
花椒粒、小茴各¹/₄小匙
甘草 1片

2
麻油、黑醋 各1小匙
味精 .... ¹/₈小匙

1　黃豆芽洗淨入鍋燙熟，隨即撈起瀝乾；豆包切絲，青蒜、紅辣椒洗淨切斜片備用。
2　鍋熱入油2大匙燒熱，入青蒜、辣椒及薑片爆香，續入 **1** 料煮開，改小火煮至湯汁剩¹/₂ 杯時（約30分鐘），撈去殘渣，再入黃豆芽及豆包拌炒均勻，隨即盛起，待涼，入 **2** 料拌勻即可。

---

1 lb. (450 g) soy bean sprouts
2²/₃ oz. (80 g) fried bean curd pouch
1 stalk fresh garlic
1 red chili pepper
1 slice ginger root

1
1¹/₂ C. water
2 T. soy sauce
2 t. crystal sugar
¹/₄ t. each: fennel,Szechwan peppercorns
1 piece licorice

2 1t. each: sesame oil, black vinegar

1　Wash the soy bean sprouts, scald briefly in boiling water, remove and drain. Cut the fried bean curd pouch into julienne strips. Wash the fresh garlic and the red chili pepper, cut both into diagonal slices.
2　Heat a wok, add 2T. oil. Stir-fry the garlic leek, red chili pepper, and ginger until fragrant. Add **1** and bring to a boil, reduce to low heat and simmer until the sauce reduces to ¹/₂C. (about 30 minutes). Strain the sauce and add the soy bean sprouts and bean curd pouch. Stir-fry, mix well, remove and arrange on a plate. Cool, season with **2** and serve.

拌干絲
Bean Curd Strips Salad

干絲（處理過）.. 200公克　芹菜（淨重）........ 40公克
紅辣椒 .... ¹/₂條

1
麻油 3大匙
鹽 .... ³/₄小匙
味精 .... ¹/₄小匙

1　干絲切段；芹菜洗淨，切5公分段後拍裂並撕成細絲；紅辣椒洗淨、去籽切絲備用。
2　干絲與芹菜分別用開水川燙後，泡入冷開水中漂涼，撈出瀝乾。
3　將干絲、芹菜、紅辣椒絲與 **1** 料拌勻即可。

---

7 oz. (200 g) bean curd strips (processed)
1¹/₃ oz. (40 g) Chinese celery (net weight)
¹/₂ red chili pepper

1
3 T. sesame oil
³/₄ t. salt

1　Cut the bean curd strips into sections. Wash celery, cut into 5 cm (2") sections and shred. Wash red chili pepper, discard the seeds and shred.
2　Blanch the bean curd strips and celery separately in boiling water. Rinse under cold water to cool and drain.
3　Mix the bean curd strips, celery, red chili pepper, and **1** well. Serve.

紅燒烤麩
Soy-Simmered Bran Puffs

冬筍	300公克	烤麩	120公克
胡蘿蔔	80公克	豆干	70公克
厚香菇（小朵）....	10公克		

1
- 水 2杯
- 醬油 4大匙
- 麻油、薑汁 各1大匙
- 糖 2小匙

1 烤麩切０·５公分之厚片，冬筍去殼洗淨，胡蘿蔔亦洗淨去皮，均切０·５×２×３公分之厚片；香菇泡軟洗淨去蒂，豆干每塊切成４等份。
2 鍋熱入油６杯燒至七分熱（約１６０℃），入烤麩炸至金黃色後，撈起瀝油備用。
3 **1**料入鍋煮開，入冬筍、胡蘿蔔、豆干及香菇，以中火先燒１０分鐘，再入烤麩改小火煮至湯汁快收乾即可。

$^2/_3$ lb. (300 g) bamboo shoots
$4^1/_4$ oz. (120 g) gluten puffs
$2^2/_3$ oz. (80 g) carrot
$2^1/_3$ oz. (70 g) pressed bean curds
$^1/_3$ oz. (10 g) small,thick dried chinese black mush-
        rooms

1
- 2 C. water
- 4 T. soy sauce
- 1 T. each: sesame oil, ginger root juice
- 2 t. sugar

1 Cut the gluten puffs into 0.5cm ($^1/_4$") slices. Husk the bamboo shoots and wash. Peel the carrot and wash. Cut both bamboo shoots and carrot into 0.5 x 2 x 3cm ($^1/_4$"x$^3/_4$"x1$^1/_4$") slices. Soak the dried mushrooms until soft and remove the stems. Cut each piece of pressed bean curd into 4 equal pieces.
2 Heat a wok. Add 6C.oil and heat to about 160°C (320°F). Deep-fry the gluten puffs until golden. Remove from the oil and drain.
3 Bring **1** to a boil in a wok. Add the bamboo shoots, carrot, pressed bean curds and black mushrooms. Cook 10 minutes over medium heat. Add the gluten puffs and cook over low heat until the sauce is almost evaporated. Serve.

茼蒿拌豆干
Garland Chrysanthemum Salad

茼蒿菜	300公克	小豆干	5塊

1
- 麻油 .... 1$^1/_3$大匙
- 鹽 .... $^1/_2$小匙
- 味精 .... $^1/_4$小匙

1 茼蒿洗淨，入開水川燙後，以冷水漂涼並擠乾水份，切碎；豆干亦川燙漂涼後，切成小細片。
2 茼蒿、豆干加**1**料拌勻即可。

$^2/_3$ lb. (300 g) garland chrysanthemum
5 pieces small pressed bean curds

1
- 1$^1/_3$ T. sesame oil
- $^1/_2$ t. salt

1 Wash garland chrysanthemum, parboil in boiling water. Rinse under cold water to cool, squeeze off water and chop. Repeat the process with the bean curds, parboil, cool, then dice.
2 Mix garland chrysanthemum, bean curds, and **1** well . Serve.

滷花生
Braised Soy Peanuts

花生 180公克

1
水 6杯
小蘇打 .... $^1/_2$小匙

2
花椒粒 1小匙
小茴 .... $^1/_4$小匙
桂皮（拍碎）.. $^1/_8$小匙
八角 1顆

3
紅辣椒 .... $^1/_2$條
蔥 4段
薑 2片
蒜頭 2粒

4
醬油 4大匙
酒 1大匙
糖 2小匙
鹽 .... $^1/_4$小匙

1　花生洗淨，泡水２４小時後瀝乾，入**1**料中煮１$^1/_2$小時（如果水不夠，須再加水），撈起，入冷水中浸泡，期間每隔數分鐘換水一次，至去除蘇打味後，再瀝乾水份，並將**2**料裝入滷包袋中綁緊備用。
2　鍋熱入油２大匙燒熱，入**3**料爆香，再入水３杯及**2**料煮開，改小火加蓋燜煮３０分鐘後，入花生及**4**料加蓋續煮至剩約１杯水時（約１５分鐘），熄火再燜３０分鐘即可。

6$^1/_6$ oz. (180 g) fresh peanuts

1
6 C. water
$^1/_2$ t. baking soda

2
1 t. Szechwan peppercorns
$^1/_4$ t. fennel
$^1/_8$ t. cinnamon (crushed)
1 star anise

3
$^1/_2$ red chili pepper
4 sections green onion (1$^1/_4$")
2 slices ginger root
2 garlic cloves

4
4 T. soy sauce
1 T. cooking wine
2 t. sugar
$^1/_4$ t. salt

1　Wash peanuts and soak in water for 24 hours, drain. Boil peanuts in **1** for 1$^1/_2$ hours (add more water if necessary), drain. Soak in cold water, change water every few minutes to get rid of the soda taste, drain. Place **2** into a spice pouch.
2　Heat the wok, add 2T.oil. Stir-fry **3** until fragrant. Add 3C. water and spice pouch. Bring to a boil. Cover with a lid and simmer over low heat for 30 minutes. Add the peanuts and **4**, cover, continue to simmer until sauce reduces to 1C. (about 15 minutes). Turn off the heat and let stand for 30 minutes. Serve.

毛豆豆干
Savory Fresh Soybeans

熟毛豆仁、小豆干 ....
.... 各150公克

1
糖、醬油 各1大匙
鹽 .... $^1/_2$小匙
味精 .... $^1/_4$小匙

1　毛豆仁洗淨瀝乾，豆干亦洗淨切小丁備用。
2　鍋熱入油３大匙，入毛豆仁、豆干丁及**1**料拌炒均勻即可。

5$^1/_4$ oz. (150 g) each: boiled fresh soybeans,
small pressed bean curds

1
1 T. each: sugar, soy sauce
$^1/_2$ t. salt

1　Wash boiled fresh soybeans and drain. Wash pressed bean curds and dice.
2　Heat the wok, add 3T. oil. Stir-fry fresh soybeans, diced bean curds and **1**. Mix well and serve.

辣白菜
Spicy Cabbage

高麗菜	300公克	麻油	1½大匙
鹽	1½小匙	辣椒醬	1小匙
花椒粒	½小匙		

1 紅辣椒絲 .... 1大匙　**2** 糖、白醋 各1½大匙
　　薑絲、蒜末 .. 各½小匙

1 高麗菜洗淨切細絲，入鹽醃20分鐘，再入冷開水漂洗
　擠乾後，灑上**1**料備用。
2 鍋熱入麻油燒熱，入花椒以小火略炒後撈出，續入辣椒
　醬炒香，再入**2**料炒勻，隨即倒在高麗菜上拌勻，冷藏
　30分鐘使之入味即可。

■高麗菜可以大白菜300公克取代。

2/3 lb. (300 g) cabbage
1½ T. sesame oil
1½ t. salt
1 t. hot chili paste
½ t. Szechwan peppercorns

1 1 T. shredded red chili pepper
　　 ½ T. each: shredded ginger roots,
　　　　　　　minced garlic cloves

2 1½ T. each: sugar, white vinegar

1 Wash cabbage and shred fine. Marinate with salt
  for 20 minutes, rinse under cold water and
  squeeze off excess water. Sprinkle on **1**.
2 Heat a wok. Add sesame oil, stir-fry Szechwan
  peppercorns slightly and remove. Stir in hot chili
  paste and stir-fry until fragrant. Mix in **2** well.
  Pour over cabbage and mix well. Refrigerate for
  30 minutes and serve.
■ Cabbage may be replaced by 10½ oz.(300g) of
  nappa cabbage.

辣白菜 · *Spicy Cabbage*

辣拌大頭菜 · *Spicy Chinese Turnip*

辣拌大頭菜
Spicy Chinese Turnip

大頭菜（1顆）	600公克	鹽	2小匙

1 麻油 2大匙
　　 辣豆瓣醬 1大匙
　　 糖、醬油 各1小匙
　　 鹽、味精 .... 各¼小匙

1 大頭菜洗淨，去皮及粗纖維，橫切成兩半後，切細薄
　片，加鹽拌醃至軟（約10分鐘）。
2 結頭菜漂洗去鹽，再以冷開水沖洗後，擠乾水份，入**1**
　料拌勻即可。

1⅓ lb. (600 g) Chinese turnip (one whole)
2 t. salt

1 2 T. sesame oil
　　 1 T. chili bean paste
　　 1 t. each: sugar, soy sauce
　　 ¼ t. salt

1 Wash Chinese turnip, pare off the skin and discard the tough outer fibers. Cut in half width-
  wise, then cut into thin slices. Marinate with salt
  until soft (about 10 minutes).
2 Rinse salt off Chinese turnip and squeeze off excess water. Mix well with **1** and serve.

銀魚空心菜
On-choy in Fish Sauce

空心菜梗 .... 200公克　蒜末 1大匙

1⎰ 銀魚 .... 35公克　**2** 糖、味精 ...... 各 $^1/_4$ 小匙
　　豆豉 1大匙
　　紅辣椒丁 .... $1^1/_2$ 小匙

1　空心菜梗洗淨切小丁，銀魚、豆豉洗淨瀝乾備用。
2　鍋熱入油4大匙燒熱，入蒜末爆香，再入**1**料拌炒，最
　後入空心菜梗及**2**料快炒數下即可。

---

7 oz. (200 g) on-choy stems
1 T. minced garlic cloves
$^1/_4$ t. sugar

1⎰ **$1^1/_4$ oz. (35 g) small silver fish**
　1 T. fermented black beans
　$1^1/_2$ t. diced red chili pepper

1　Wash on-choy stems and dice. Wash silver fish
　and fermented black beans, drain.
2　Heat the wok, add 4T. oil. Stir-fry minced garlic
　cloves until fragrant. Add **1**, stir-fry and mix well.
　Then add diced on-choy stems and season with
　$^1/_4$ t. sugar, stir-fry and mix well. Serve.

廣東泡菜・ *Cantonese Pickles*

廣東泡菜
Cantonese Pickles

白蘿蔔 .... 220公克　胡蘿蔔 100公克
小黃瓜 .... 80公克　紅辣椒 .... $^1/_2$ 條
鹽 .... $^1/_2$ 大匙　薑 10片

1 糖、白醋 各3大匙

1　白蘿蔔、胡蘿蔔洗淨去皮切滾刀塊，小黃瓜洗淨亦切滾
　刀塊，一起入鹽醃約6小時；紅辣椒洗淨切細環狀。
2　將醃好的白蘿蔔、胡蘿蔔、小黃瓜以水漂去鹽份（約5
　分鐘），再以冷開水沖洗並擦乾水份後，入薑片、紅辣
　椒及**1**料拌勻，醃約3小時即可。

$7^2/_3$ oz. (220 g) turnip
$3^1/_2$ oz. (100 g) carrots
3 oz. (80 g) gherkin cucumbers
$^1/_2$ red chili pepper
10 slices ginger root
$^1/_2$ T. salt

1 **3 T. each: sugar, white vinegar**

1　Wash turnip and carrots, pare off the skin and
　cut both into diagonal pieces. Wash cucumbers
　and cut into diagonal pieces. Marinate all three
　together with salt for about 6 hours. Wash red
　chili pepper and slice into thin rings.
2　Rinse turnip,carrots, and cucumbers under cold
　water for about 5 minutes to get rid of salt, drain,
　and pat dry. Mix with ginger roots, red chili pep-
　per and **1**. Pickle for 3 hours and serve.

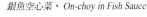

銀魚空心菜・ *On-choy in Fish Sauce*

四川泡菜
Szechwan Pickled Cabbage

高麗菜 .... 460公克　紅辣椒 5條

1
┌ 冷開水 5杯
│ 鹽 1大匙
│ 花椒粒 1小匙
└ 味精 ³/4小匙

1 高麗菜一片片剝下洗淨，紅辣椒洗淨切小段，均風乾水份（約1／2天）備用。

2 玻璃罐洗淨，擦乾水份，入**1**料、高麗菜及紅辣椒浸泡，將容器口蓋緊，置於室溫內發酵即可。

■ 發酵時間長短之判斷，以食用高麗菜葉梗判定，無生澀味即可（約3天），且發酵好即撈出放置冷藏，否則會太酸，餘汁亦可回收再利用。

■ 除高麗菜外，亦可泡白蘿蔔，處理方法如下：白蘿蔔洗淨縱切成4～6瓣，風乾至軟（約1天），再加入浸泡即可。

1 lb. (460 g) cabbage
5 red chili peppers

1
┌ **5 C. water**
│ **1 T. salt**
└ **1 t. Szechwan peppercorns**

1 Peel the cabbage leaves off one by one and wash. Wash red chili peppers and cut into small sections . Leave both to dry in an airy place (about ¹/₂ day).

2 Pour **1** into a clean, dry glass jar. Add cabbage leaves and red chili peppers. Close the jar tightly and leave at room temperature to ferment.

■ Length of fermentation depends on the taste of the cabbage stem. It is considered ready when there is no bitter taste (about 3 days). Cabbage should be removed as soon as fermentation is done, or else cabbage will become too sour. The juice may be re-used again.

■ Besides cabbage, turnip may be used. The method is as follows: Wash the turnip and cut into 4 to 6 serving pieces. Air dry to soften (about 1 day), add it to the juice to ferment.

韓國泡菜
Korean Kimchi

大白菜 .... 900公克　鹽 2大匙

1
┌ 蒜末 2大匙
│ 薑末 1大匙
└ 紅辣椒末 2小匙

2
┌ 蔥末、辣椒粉各1¹/2大匙
│ 糖 1小匙
└ 味精 ¹/4小匙

1 大白菜洗淨切成5公分段，入鹽醃至菜葉變軟出水後（約4小時），以冷水漂洗至鹹味適中，擠乾水份備用。

2 **1**料用刀背搗碎，與**2**料混合均勻並入大白菜拌勻後，放入容器內蓋緊蓋子，置陰涼處隔天即可。

■ 為避免酸味太強，醃泡1-2天後應置冰箱冷藏

2 lb. (900 g) nappa cabbage
2 T. salt

1
┌ **2 T. minced garlic cloves**
│ **1 T. minced ginger roots**
└ **2 t. minced red chili pepper**

2
┌ **1¹/2 T. each: minced green onion,**
│ **　　　　　　red chili pepper powder**
└ **1 t. sugar**

1 Wash cabbage and cut into 5 cm (2") serving sections. Marinate with salt until leaves soften and liquid forms (about 4 hours). Rinse off excess salt. Squeeze dry.

2 Mash the ingredients together in **1** and mix well with **2** . Add cabbage and mix well. Place in a clean dry glass jar and seal tightly. Leave the jar in a cool place overnight. Serve.

■ The cabbage should be refrigerated after marinating for 1-2 days to avoid becoming too sour.

上海泡菜
Shanghai Pickled Cabbage

高麗菜	1200公克	紅辣椒	2條
蒜頭	2粒	鹽	2大匙

1
- 紹興酒 1大匙
- 糖 1½小匙
- 鹽 1小匙
- 花椒粒 .... ½小匙

1 高麗菜洗淨，用手撕成適當大小後，瀝乾水份，紅辣椒洗淨去籽切斜段，蒜頭洗淨拍碎去皮。

2 取一乾淨容器，先鋪上一層高麗菜，灑上一層鹽，再鋪上一層菜，再灑上一層鹽，如此依序將材料鋪完，醃至略為出水即可（約30分鐘，期間要翻動使醃漬均勻）。

3 6杯涼開水中入**1**料、紅辣椒及蒜頭後，再入瀝乾之高麗菜，蓋上保鮮膜或蓋子，冷藏1天即可。

2²/₃ lb. (1200 g) cabbage
2 red chili peppers
2 garlic cloves
2 T. salt

1
- **1 T. Chinese Shao-Shing wine**
- **1½ t. sugar**
- **1 t. salt**
- **½ t. Szechwan peppercorns**

1 Wash cabbage, tear into serving pieces by hand, pat dry with kitchen towel. Wash red chili peppers, discard the seeds and cut into diagonal sections. Rinse garlic cloves, peel off the skin and crush with the back of a knife.

2 In a clean container, spread one layer of cabbage, sprinkle a layer of salt, then spread another layer of cabbage and salt until all cabbage and salt are used. Marinate until some liquid forms at the bottom (about 30 minutes). Cabbage must be turned sometimes during the marinating period to evenly distribute the taste.

3 Add **1**, red chili peppers, and garlic cloves into 6C. cold water, then add drained cabbage. Cover with plastic wrap or a lid. Refrigerate for one day and serve cold.

涼拌黃瓜
Cucumber Salad

小黃瓜	400公克	紅辣椒	2條
蒜頭	4粒	鹽	1小匙

1
- 麻油 1½大匙
- 白醋 2小匙
- 糖 1小匙
- 味精 .... ¼小匙

1 小黃瓜洗淨去頭尾，切成4段後拍碎，入鹽拌醃至出水（約20分鐘）；紅辣椒洗淨切斜片，蒜頭洗淨去皮拍碎備用。

2 小黃瓜瀝去水份，入**1**料、蒜頭及辣椒拌勻，再入冰箱冷藏30分鐘即可。

14 oz. (400 g) gherkin cucumbers
2 red chili peppers
4 garlic cloves
1 t. salt

1
- **1½ T. sesame oil**
- **2 t. white vinegar**
- **1 t. sugar**

1 Wash gherkin cucumbers and trim off both ends. Cut into 4 sections and crush with the back of a knife. Mix with salt and marinate until liquid forms (about 20 minutes). Wash red chili peppers and cut into diagonal slices. Wash garlic cloves and peel off the skin, crush with the back of a knife.

2 Drain excess liquid from cucumbers. Mix well with **1**, garlic cloves, and red chili peppers. Refrigerate for 30 minutes and serve.

酸辣黃瓜
Spicy and Sour Cucumber

小黃瓜	400公克	麻油		2大匙
辣豆瓣醬	1²/₃大匙	蒜末		1大匙
鹽	1小匙			

1
- 白醋 1¹/₂大匙
- 糖 2¹/₂小匙
- 味精 .... ¹/₈小匙

1　小黃瓜洗淨去頭尾，切3公分段後拍碎，入鹽拌醃至出水（約20分鐘），瀝乾水份備用。
2　鍋熱入麻油燒熱，入蒜末爆香，再入辣豆瓣醬拌勻，熄火放涼後，入**1**料與小黃瓜拌勻即可。

---

1 lb. (450 g) gherkin cucumbers
2 T. sesame oil
1²/₃ T. chili bean paste
1 T. minced garlic cloves
1 t. salt

1
1¹/₂ T. white vinegar
2¹/₂ T. sugar

1　Wash gherkin cucumbers and trim off both ends. Cut into 3 cm (1") sections and crush with the back of a knife. Mix with salt and marinate until liquid forms (about 20 minutes). Drain excess liquid from the cucumbers.
2　Heat a wok. Add sesame oil and stir-fry minced garlic cloves until fragrant. Mix in chili bean paste well. Turn off the heat and cool. Mix in **1** and gherkin cucumbers evenly. Serve.

麻辣黃瓜 • *Peppery Cucumber*

麻辣黃瓜
Peppery Cucumber

小黃瓜	300克	乾辣椒		5條
麻油	2大匙	鹽、花椒粒		各1小匙

1
- 薑絲、紅辣椒絲 各10公克

2 白醋、糖 各1大匙

1　乾辣椒切2公分段，去籽；小黃瓜洗淨去頭尾，視大小對剖成4或6條，去籽切成5公分長段，加鹽拌醃至出水（約20分鐘），再以冷開水沖洗瀝乾，入大碗內，灑上**1**料備用。
2　鍋熱入麻油燒熱，入乾辣椒以中小火爆香，再入花椒粒略炒（約30秒），趁熱沖淋在薑絲、紅辣椒絲上，再加**2**料拌勻，冷藏醃約3小時即可。

---

²/₃ lb. (300 g) gherkin cucumbers
5 dried red chili peppers
2 T. sesame oil
1 t. each: salt, Szechwan peppercorns

1
10 g (¹/₂ oz.) each: shredded ginger roots,
shredded red chili pepper

2 **1 T. each: white vinegar, sugar**

1　Cut dried red chili peppers into 2 cm (1") sections and discard the seeds. Wash gherkin cucumbers and trim off both ends. Cut lengthwise in 4 or 6 long strips, scoop out the seeds, and cut into 5 cm (2") sections. Marinate with salt until liquid forms (about 20 minutes). Rinse under cold water, drain. Place gherkin cucumbers in a large bowl, sprinkle on **1**.
2　Heat the wok, add sesame oil. Stir-fry shredded dried red chili peppers over low heat until fragrant. Add peppercorns to fry slightly (about 30 seconds). While hot, pour over shredded ginger and shredded red chili pepper. Season with **2** and mix well. Refrigerate for 3 hours and serve.

酸辣黃瓜 • *Spicy and Sour Cucumber*

涼拌西芹
Celery Salad

西芹（淨重）...... 300公克

1
┌ 榨菜末 3大匙
└ 蝦米 1½小匙

2
┌ 麻油 1大匙
│ 醬油 .... ½大匙
└ 鹽、味精、糖各¼小匙

1 蝦米洗淨切末；鍋熱入油1大匙燒熱，入**1**料炒香後，盛起待涼備用。

2 西芹洗淨去老纖維、切斜片，入開水中川燙30秒，取出，入冷開水中漂涼，撈起瀝乾後，再入**1**、**2**料拌勻即可。

---

²/₃ lb. (300 g) celery (net weight)

1
┌ 3 T. minced Szechwan pickled mustard greens
└ 1½ t. dried baby shrimp

2
┌ 1 T. sesame oil
│ ½ T. soy sauce
└ ¼ t. each: salt, sugar

1 Wash dried baby shrimp and mince. Heat a wok. Add 1T. oil, stir-fry **1** until fragrant, remove and cool.

2 Wash and remove the tough strings from the celery, cut into diagonal slices, and scald in boiling water for 30 seconds. Remove and rinse under cold water to cool, drain. Mix celery well with **1** and **2**. Serve.

涼拌西芹・ Celery Salad

涼拌茄段・ Ginger Flavored Eggplant

涼拌茄段
Ginger Flavored Eggplant

茄子 .... 300公克   薑泥 2小匙

1
┌ 醬油 2大匙
│ 麻油 1小匙
└ 味精 .... ¼小匙

1 茄子洗淨，切5公分長段。

2 水6杯煮開，入茄子煮至熟軟後，取出以冷開水漂涼，再撕成適當之條狀。

3 茄子置於盤上，上灑薑泥，食時再淋上**1**料即可。

---

²/₃ lb. (300 g) eggplant
2 t. ginger root paste

1
┌ 2 T. soy sauce
└ 1 t. sesame oil

1 Wash eggplant, cut into 5 cm (2 ") long sections.

2 Bring 6C. water to a boil, cook eggplant until soft. Rinse under cold water to cool. Shred by hand into serving strips.

3 Arrange eggplant strips on a plate, sprinkle on ginger root paste. Pour **1** over the eggplant strips before serving.

香炒茄子
Basil Flavored Eggplant

茄子	300公克	九層塔	30公克
紅辣椒	1條	蒜頭	2粒

1
水	⅓杯
醬油	1⅓大匙
糖	1 小匙
鹽	⅓小匙

1 茄子洗淨切滾刀塊，入冷水中浸泡；九層塔去梗洗淨；紅辣椒洗淨去籽切片，蒜頭洗淨拍碎備用。
2 鍋熱入油 2½大匙燒熱，入蒜頭爆香，續入瀝乾之茄子拌炒至表面微焦，再入 **1** 料以小火煮至茄子軟化（約3分鐘），最後入九層塔及紅辣椒拌勻即可。

⅔ lb. (300 g) eggplant
1 oz. (30 g) fresh basil
1 red chili pepper
2 garlic cloves

1
⅓ C. water
1⅓ T. soy sauce
1 t. sugar
⅓ t. salt

1 Wash eggplant, cut into diagonal pieces, and soak in cold water. Wash fresh basil and discard the stems. Wash red chili pepper, discard the seeds and slice. Wash garlic cloves, peel off the skin and crush with the back of a knife.
2 Heat the wok, add 2½ T. oil. Stir-fry garlic cloves until fragrant. Add drained eggplant and stir-fry until the skin is slightly scorched. Pour in **1** and simmer over low heat until eggplant is tender (about 3 minutes). Mix in basil leaves and red chili pepper. Serve.

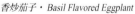

香炒茄子・ *Basil Flavored Eggplant*

雪菜豆芽・ *Tasty Soy Bean Sprouts*

雪菜豆芽
Tasty Soy Bean Sprouts

黃豆芽	300公克	黃雪菜	150公克
紅辣椒	2條	麻油	1小匙

1
鹽	½小匙
味精	¼小匙

1 黃豆芽洗淨去根；黃雪菜洗淨切末；紅辣椒洗淨去籽、切絲備用。
2 鍋熱入油2大匙燒熱，入紅辣椒爆香，續入雪菜、黃豆芽拌炒，至黃豆芽稍軟時（約5分鐘），入 **1** 料調味，最後入麻油拌勻即可。

⅔ lb. (300 g) soy bean sprouts
5⅓ oz. (150 g) yellow pickled mustard greens
2 red chili peppers
1 t. sesame oil
½ t. salt

1 Wash soy bean sprouts and snip off the ends. Wash and mince yellow pickled mustard greens. Wash red chili peppers, discard the seeds and shred.
2 Heat a wok, add 2T. oil. Stir-fry red chili pepper until fragrant. Add yellow pickled mustard greens and soy bean sprouts. Stir-fry until soy bean sprouts soften (about 5 minutes). Season with salt, mix well with sesame oil. Serve.

素拉皮
Cucumber in Sesame Sauce

小黃瓜 .... 200公克　粉皮 170公克
麻油 .... 2小匙　鹽 .... ³/₄小匙

1
蔥末 1¹/₃大匙
芝麻醬 、麻油 、冷高湯
.... 各 2小匙
醬油、糖 各1¹/₂小匙
鹽 .... ¹/₈小匙

1　小黃瓜洗淨去頭尾，切薄片，入鹽拌醃至出水後（20
　分鐘），擠乾水份，置盤底。
2　粉皮切條狀，以熱開水沖燙過，瀝乾水份，再入麻油拌
　勻，待涼置黃瓜上。
3　將**1**料拌勻，食時淋於粉皮上拌勻即可。

---

7 oz. (200 g) gherkin cucumbers
6 oz. (170 g) mung bean sheets
2 t. sesame oil
³/₄ t. salt

1
1¹/₃ T. minced green onion
2 t. each: sesame paste, sesame oil, cold stock
1¹/₂ t. each: soy sauce, sugar
¹/₈ t. salt

1　Wash cucumbers and trim off both ends, slice
　thin. Marinate with salt until liquid forms (about
　20 minutes). Drain excess water and arrange on
　a plate.
2　Cut mung bean sheets into long strips, scald in
　boiling water, drain. Mix with sesame oil, cool.
　Arrange on top of the cucumbers.
3　Mix all the ingredients in **1** well. Pour the sauce
　over mung bean sheets before serving.

開陽香蒜・ *Appetizing Garlic Leek*

開陽香蒜
Appetizing Garlic Leek

蒜苗 .... 180公克　蝦米（²/₃杯）...... 60公克
紅辣椒 .... 1條　糖 .... ¹/₂小匙

1　蝦米洗淨瀝乾，切成細丁，青蒜洗淨亦切成小片；紅辣
　椒洗淨去籽切小片備用。
2　鍋熱入油３大匙燒熱，入蝦米及紅辣椒炒香，再入蒜
　苗、糖拌炒數下即可。

6¹/₂ oz. (180 g) fresh garlic
2 oz. (60 g) dried baby shrimp
1 red chili pepper
¹/₂ t. sugar

1　Wash shrimp and pat dry, finely dice. Wash fresh
　garlic and dice. Wash red chili pepper, discard
　the seeds and dice.
2　Heat a wok, add 3T. oil. Stir-fry shrimp and red
　chili pepper until fragrant. Add fresh garlic and
　sugar, stir-fry until well-mixed. Serve.

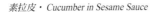

素拉皮・ *Cucumber in Sesame Sauce*

炒三鮮
Gourmet Bamboo

熟筍 .... 180公克　中式火腿（淨重）　40公克
干貝 .... 2粒　酒 1小匙

1⌈水 .... ¹/₂杯
　└太白粉 .... ³/₄ 小匙

1　筍切細絲；中式火腿洗淨，入鍋蒸熟（約１５分鐘），
　　取出待涼切絲；干貝加水２大匙入鍋蒸軟（約１５分
　　鐘），取出待涼拆絲，餘汁留用。
2　鍋熱入油２大匙燒熱，入火腿炒香，續入筍絲及**1**料炒
　　勻且煮開，再入干貝、干貝蒸汁及酒炒勻即可。

■　此道菜可以培根８０公克取代中式火腿，另加鹽¹/₄小匙
　　調味，其餘材料及做法相同。

6¹/₄ oz. (180 g) boiled bamboo shoots
1¹/₃ oz. (40 g) Chinese ham (net weight)
2 dried scallops
1 t. cooking wine

1⌈¹/₂ C. water
　└³/₄ t. cornstarch

1　Shred bamboo shoots . Wash ham and steam
　　(about 15 minutes), remove, cool, then shred.
　　Add 2T. water to dried scallops and steam until
　　tender (about 15 minutes), remove, cool and then
　　shred by hand. Reserve the water for later use.
2　Heat a wok, add 2T. oil. Stir-fry ham until fra-
　　grant, add shredded bamboo shoots and **1**. Bring
　　the sauce to a boil, then add shredded scallops,
　　reserved water, and cooking wine. Mix well and
　　serve.

■　Chinese ham may be replaced by 2³/₄ oz. (80 g)
　　bacon, seasoned with ¹/₄ t. salt. Proceed with re-
　　maining ingredients and methods as directed,
　　above,

炒三鮮・ *Gourmet Bamboo*

糖醋白蘿蔔・ *Sweet and Sour Turnips*

糖醋白蘿蔔
Sweet and Sour Turnips

白蘿蔔 .... 400公克　紅辣椒 1條
鹽 1大匙

1⌈白醋 3大匙
　│糖 2¹/₂大匙
　│花椒粒 .... ¹/₂小匙
　└鹽 .... ¹/₈小匙

1　白蘿蔔洗淨去皮切細薄片，加鹽拌醃至軟後（約２０分
　　鐘），漂去鹽份，再以冷開水沖過，擠乾水份；紅辣椒
　　去籽切片備用。
2　將白蘿蔔、紅辣椒及**1**料拌勻，醃約４小時即可。
■　糖醋高麗菜：以高麗菜４００公克取代白蘿蔔，洗淨切
　　小片，其餘材料及做法同糖醋白蘿蔔。

---

1 lb. (450 g) turnip
1 red chili pepper
1 T. salt

1⌈3 T. white vinegar
　│2¹/₂ T. sugar
　│¹/₂ t. Szechwan peppercorns
　└¹/₈ t. salt

1　Wash turnip, peel off the skin and slice thinly.
　　Marinate with salt until soft (about 20 minutes).
　　Rinse off the salt and squeeze off excess water.
　　Discard the seeds in red chili pepper and slice.
2　Mix turnip, red chili pepper, and **1** well. Mari-
　　nate for about 4 hours. Serve.
■　Sweet and Sour Cabbage: Replace turnip with
　　cabbage (400 g or 14 oz.). Wash cabbage and
　　cut into small serving pieces. Proceed with re-
　　maining ingredients and methods as directed,
　　above.

菜心豆干
Cabbage Salad

大白菜（取粗梗）300公克　小豆干 100公克
香菜葉 .... ½杯　蔥（淨重） 40公克

1
麻油、白醋 各2大匙
醬油 1⅓大匙
糖 2小匙
鹽 .... ½小匙

1　大白菜洗淨切細絲；小豆干洗淨，橫切成3至4片，再切細絲，入開水中川燙，撈起瀝乾水份待涼；蔥洗淨切細絲，泡水至蔥絲捲起後（約5分鐘），去水備用。
2　將白菜絲、豆乾絲、蔥絲、香菜葉及**1**料拌勻即可。

²⁄₃ lb. (300 g) nappa cabbage (stem parts only)
3½ oz. (100 g) small pressed bean curd
½ C. coriander leaves
1⅓ oz. (40 g) green onions (net weight)

1
2 T. each: sesame oil, white vinegar
1⅓ T. soy sauce
2 t. sugar
½ t. salt

1　Wash cabbage, drain and shred fine. Wash small pressed bean curd, cut into 3 to 4 horizontal slices, then shred. Blanch in boiling water, drain and cool. Wash green onions and shred. Soak in water until green onion shreds curl up (about 5 minutes), drain.
2　Mix cabbage, bean curd, green onions, coriander leaves and **1** together. Serve.

乾煸筍・ Dry-Fried Bamboo Shoots

乾煸筍
Dry-Fried Bamboo Shoots

綠竹筍（淨重） .. 300公克

1
蝦米末、榨菜末、絞肉
 .... 各1大匙

2
酒 2大匙
蔥末 1大匙
糖 1小匙
鹽 .... ½小匙
味精 .... ¼小匙

1　綠竹筍洗淨，切5公分長條狀；鍋熱入油4杯燒至七分熱（約160℃），入綠竹筍炸至黃褐色後，撈起瀝油備用。
2　另鍋熱入油2大匙燒熱，入**1**料炒香，續入筍塊炒勻，再入**2**料炒至湯汁收乾即可。

²⁄₃ lb. (300 g) fresh bamboo shoots (net weight)

1
1 T. each: minced dried baby shrimp,
　　　minced Szechwan pickled mustard-
　　　greens , ground pork

2
2 T. cooking wine
1 T. minced green onion
1 t. sugar
½ t. salt

1　Wash fresh bamboo shoots, cut into 5 cm long strips. Heat a wok. Add 4C. oil and heat to 160°C (320°F). Deep-fry bamboo shoots until golden brown. Remove and drain.
2　In another wok, add 2T. oil. Stir-fry **1** until fragrant, stir in bamboo shoots and mix well. Add **2** and stir-fry until the sauce has evaporated. Serve.

菜心豆干・ Cabbage Salad

香炒箭筍
Minced Pork and Bamboo Shoots

箭筍 .... 200公克　絞肉 110公克
紅辣椒 .... 1條　蔥 10段

1
水 1杯
醬油、糖 各2小匙
鹽 1/2小匙
味精 1/8小匙

1　箭筍洗淨切5公分段；紅辣椒洗淨去籽切片備用。
2　水5杯煮開，入箭筍煮約5分鐘以去除酸味後，撈起瀝乾。
3　鍋熱入油1大匙燒熱，入絞肉炒熟，續入紅辣椒、蔥段炒香，再入箭筍及**1**料，改小火加蓋燜煮約10分鐘，最後開大火將湯汁收乾即可。

7 oz. (200 g) small bamboo shoots
3²/₃ oz. (110 g) ground pork
1 red chili pepper
10 sections green onion (1¹/₄")

1
1 C. water
2 t. each: soy sauce, sugar
1/₂ t. salt

1　Wash small bamboo shoots. Wash red chili pepper , discard the seeds and slice.
2　Bring 5C. water to a boil, add bamboo shoots and boil for 5 minutes. Remove and drain.
3　Heat a wok, add 1T. oil. Stir-fry ground pork until brown. Add red chili pepper and green onion sections, stir-fry until fragrant. Stir in bamboo shoots and **1**, turn heat to low and cover with a lid, simmer for 10 minutes. Remove the lid, cook over high heat until sauce is completely evaporated. Serve warm or cold.

炒桂竹筍
Stir-Fried Bamboo Shoots

桂竹筍 .... 450公克　五花肉 40公克
紅辣椒 1條

1
蔥末 2大匙
蒜末 2小匙

2
醬油露 2小匙
麻油、味精 .. 各1/2小匙

1　桂竹筍洗淨，撕成細條狀後，再切成6公分段；豬肉切絲；紅辣椒洗淨去籽切絲備用。
2　鍋熱入油1/3杯燒熱，入**1**料爆香，續入肉絲、桂竹筍及辣椒拌炒均勻，再入**2**料調味即可。

1 lb. (450 g) boiled long bamboo shoots
1¹/₃ oz. (40 g) fresh bacon
1 red chili pepper

1
2 T. minced green onion
2 t. minced garlic cloves

2
2 t. soy sauce
1/₂ t. sesame oil

1　Wash long bamboo shoots, shred into thin strips and then cut into 6 cm (2¹/₂") sections. Shred fresh bacon. Wash red chili pepper, discard the seeds and shred.
2　Heat a wok, add ¹/₃ C. oil. Stir-fry **1** until fragrant. Add shredded fresh bacon, bamboo shoots, and red chili pepper. Stir-fry and mix well. Season with **2** . Serve.

紅糟肉
Scarlet Pork

五花肉 .... 300公克　地瓜粉 1/2杯

- ┌ 紅豆腐乳 1¹/₃塊
- │ 紅糟 2¹/₂大匙
- **1**│ 蒜末、酒、醬油 ....
- │ 各1¹/₃大匙
- └ 糖、太白粉 各2小匙

1. 五花肉洗淨切成4公分寬長條狀，以筷子叉洞（使醃泡時易入味），入調勻之 **1** 料醃30分鐘，再沾裹地瓜粉備用。
2. 鍋熱入油5杯燒至六分熱（140℃），入五花肉炸至熟，表皮顏色呈金黃色後撈起（約5分鐘），待涼切片即可。

---

²/₃ lb. (300 g) fresh bacon
¹/₂ C. cornstarch

- ┌ **1¹/₃ pieces preserved red bean curd**
- │ **2¹/₂ T. red fermented wine rice**
- **1**│ **1¹/₃ T. each: minced garlic cloves,**
- │ **cooking wine, soy sauce**
- └ **2 t. each: sugar, cornstarch**

1. Wash bacon, cut into 4 cm (1¹/₂") long strips, and pierce with a chopstick. Mix all the ingredients in **1** well. Marinate the meat for 30 minutes. Coat the meat with cornstarch.
2. Heat a wok. Add 5C. oil and heat to 140° C. Deep-fry the meat until golden brown (about 5 minutes). When cool, cut into slices. Serve.

蒜苗臘肉 · *Stir-Fried Chinese Bacon*

蒜苗臘肉
Stir-Fried Chinese Bacon

臘肉 .... 150公克　蒜苗 170公克
紅辣椒 1條

1 鹽、味精 ...... 各¹/₈小匙

1. 臘肉入開水中煮4分鐘，撈起，漂涼洗淨，斜切薄片；蒜苗去根及黃葉洗淨，斜切片，將蒜白與蒜葉分開；辣椒洗淨去籽切斜片備用。
2. 鍋熱入油2大匙燒熱，入臘肉炒至稍乾扁且油滲出時，入蒜白炒勻，再入蒜葉及 **1** 料拌勻即可。

■ 蒜苗炒培根：將蒜苗臘肉之臘肉以培根取代，鹽的份量視培根的鹹度而增減。

---

¹/₃ lb. (150 g) Chinese bacon
6 oz. (170 g) fresh garlic
1 red chili pepper
¹/₈ t. salt

1. Cook Chinese bacon in boiling water for 4 minutes, remove, rinse and cool. Cut into diagonal thin slices. Trim off the ends and yellow leaves of the fresh garlic. Cut into diagonal slices, separating the white and green parts. Rinse and discard the red chili pepper seeds, then cut into diagonal slices.
2. Heat a wok, add 2T. oil. Stir-fry bacon slices until fat look slightly dry. Mix in fresh garlic white part first, then mix in fresh garlic green part and salt. Serve.

■ Stir-fried Bacon: Chinese bacon may be substituted for western bacon. Amount of salt depends upon the saltiness of the bacon used.

紅糟肉 · *Scarlet Pork*

醉元寶
Drunken Pork Ingot

豬後腳 900公克

1 蔥 5段
   薑 3片

2 鹽 2小匙
   味精 .... $^1/_8$小匙
   冷高湯、紹興酒
   .... 各1$^1/_2$杯

1 豬腳洗淨，剁成2×2×3公分塊狀，入鍋中，加水及 **1** 料煮至熟爛（約1小時，煮時須維持水量蓋過豬腳）。
2 豬腳撈起瀝乾待涼，入容器內，續入 **2** 料拌勻並蓋上保鮮膜後，冷藏24小時即可。

---

2 lb. (900 g) Pork hind hoof

1 5 sections green onion (1$^1/_4$")
   3 slices ginger root

2 1$^1/_2$ C. each: cold stock, Shao-Shin wine
   2 t. salt

1 Wash the pork hind hoof, and chop into 2 x 2 x 3 cm (1"x 1"x 1$^1/_2$") pieces. Place them in a pot and cover with water and **1**. Simmer until tender (about 1 hour). Water must cover the hoof pieces during cooking.
2 Remove the hoof pieces from the pot and drain. When cool, place in a container and add **2**, mix well and cover with plastic wrap. Refrigerate for 24 hours and serve.

泡菜肉末・ Ground Pork and Pickled Cabbage

泡菜肉末
Ground Pork and Pickled Cabbage

四川泡菜(見53頁) 460公克   絞肉 250公克
紅辣椒 .... 1$^1/_2$條

1 鹽 .... $^1/_4$小匙
   味精 .... $^1/_8$小匙

1 泡菜切細絲，紅辣椒洗淨切絲。
2 鍋熱入油1$^1/_2$大匙燒熱，入絞肉炒至熟後，再入四川泡菜及 **1** 料拌炒均勻即可。

■ 泡菜肉末中之四川泡菜只取用高麗菜。
■ 四川泡高麗菜因泡的時間不同而有不同的酸度，炒時可依酸度而酌予加糖。

---

1 lb. (460 g) Szechwan Pickled Cabbage (see page 53)
8$^3/_4$ oz. (250 g) ground pork
1$^1/_2$ red chili peppers
$^1/_4$ t. salt

1 Shred pickled cabbage. Wash red chili peppers and shred.
2 Heat the wok, add 1$^1/_2$ T. oil. Stir-fry ground pork until brown, mix in pickled cabbage and salt. Stir well and serve.

■ Some pickled cabbage may be very sour. Sugar may be added to enhance the taste.

醉元寶・ Drunken Pork Ingot

肉絲拉皮
Peking Shredded Pork Appetizer

粉皮 200公克	小黃瓜 120公克
里肌肉 110公克	麻油 2小匙

1 ┌ 醬油、水、油 各2小匙
　 └ 酒 、 太白粉 各1小匙

3 芥末粉、溫開水各1大匙

2 ┌ 高湯 2大匙
　 │ 麻油 1大匙
　 │ 白醋、醬油、蔥末
　 │ 各2小匙
　 │ 芝麻醬 1¹/₂小匙
　 │ 辣油、蠔油、糖、花生
　 │ 醬 各1小匙
　 └ 薑泥 .... ¹/₂小匙

1　里肌肉切絲，入**1**料拌勻醃20分鐘；小黃瓜洗淨切細
　 絲；粉皮切1×5公分之條狀，以熱開水沖過，瀝乾，
　 再以麻油拌勻；**2**、**3**料亦分別拌勻備用。
2　鍋熱入油2大匙燒熱，入肉絲炒至熟後盛起。
3　小黃瓜置盤內，上置粉皮，再鋪上肉絲，食時拌上**2**、
　 3料即可。

---

7 oz. (200 g) mung bean sheets
4¹/₄ oz. (120 g) gherkin cucumbers
3²/₃ oz. (110 g) pork loin
2 t. sesame oil

1 ┌ 2 t. each: soy sauce, water, oil
　 └ 1 t. each: cooking wine, cornstarch

2 ┌ 2 T. stock
　 │ 1 T. sesame oil
　 │ 2 t. each: white vinegar, soy sauce,
　 │ 　　　　minced green onion
　 │ 1¹/₂ t. sesame paste
　 │ 1 t. each: chili oil, oyster sauce, sugar,
　 │ 　　　　peanut butter
　 └ ¹/₂ t. ginger paste

3 1 T. each: mustard powder, lukewarm water

1　Shred pork loin, marinate with **1** for 20 minutes.
　 Rinse gherkin cucumbers and shred into thin
　 strips. Cut mung bean sheets into 1 x 5 cm (¹/₂"x
　 2") strips. Blanch in boiling water, drain and mix
　 with sesame oil. Mix **2** and **3** in separate bowls.
2　Heat a wok, add 2T. oil. Stir-fry shredded pork
　 until brown. Remove.
3　Arrange shredded cucumbers on a plate, then ar-
　 range a layer of mung bean sheets. Spread shred-
　 ded pork on top. Mix well with **2** and **3** before
　 serving.

豉汁排骨
Pork Ribs in Black Bean Sauce

小排骨 300公克	蔥末 1大匙
太白粉 2小匙	紅辣椒末 1小匙

1 ┌ 豆豉 2大匙
　 └ 蒜末 1大匙

2 ┌ 酒 1大匙
　 │ 糖 1小匙
　 └ 醬油 1¹/₂大匙

1　排骨洗淨剁3公分長塊狀，入太白粉拌勻；豆豉洗淨備
　 用。
2　鍋熱入油1¹/₂大匙燒熱，入**1**料炒香，續入**2**料調味，
　 再入紅辣椒末拌勻，淋在排骨上，入鍋蒸50分鐘，取
　 出灑上蔥末即可。

---

²/₃ lb. (300 g) spareribs
1 T. minced green onion
2 t. cornstarch
1 t. minced red chili pepper

1 ┌ 2 T. fermented black beans
　 └ 1 T. minced garlic cloves

2 ┌ 1¹/₂ T. soy sauce
　 │ 1 T. cooking wine
　 └ 1 t. sugar

1　Wash spareribs and chop into 3 cm (1¹/₂") serv-
　 ing pieces, mix with cornstarch. Rinse black beans
　 and drain.
2　Heat a wok, add 1¹/₂T. oil. Stir-fry **1** until fra-
　 grant. Season with **2** , stir in minced red chili pep-
　 per and mix well. Pour the sauce over spareribs
　 and steam for 50 minutes. Remove and sprinkle
　 minced green onion on the top. Serve.

紅油耳絲
Spicy Pig Ear

豬耳朵（1個）.. 250公克　　蔥白 70公克
香菜末 2大匙

1
| 水 .... 6杯 |
| 蔥 .... 5段 |
| 薑 .... 2片 |
| 酒 .... 2大匙 |

2
| 辣油、醬油 各1⅓大匙 |
| 麻油 .... 1大匙 |
| 鎮江烏醋、薑末、細砂 |
| 糖 .... 各1小匙 |
| 鹽 .... ¾小匙 |

1　豬耳朵入開水川燙，撈起漂涼，用刷子或湯匙刮去表皮
　　之污垢後，洗淨瀝乾，再入煮開之**1**料以小火煮１５分
　　鐘，撈起入冰水中漂涼，瀝乾水份，切細薄片。
2　蔥白洗淨切斜片，以冷開水沖過後瀝乾水份，置於豬耳
　　朵上，再淋上調勻之**2**料拌勻，最後灑上香菜末即可。

8¾ oz. (250 g) 1 pig ear
2⅓ oz. (70 g) green onion (while part only)
2 T. minced coriander

1
- 6 C. water
- 5 sections green onion (1¼")
- 2 slices ginger root
- 2 T. cooking wine

2
- 1⅓ T. each: chili oil, soy sauce
- 1 T. sesame oil
- 1 t. each: black vinegar, minced ginger, granulated sugar
- ¾ t. salt

1　Briefly blanch pig ear in boiling water, remove
　　from water and cool. Scrape and clean carefully
　　with a brush or a spoon, rinse and drain. Bring **1**
　　to a boil. Add pig ear and simmer over low heat
　　for 15 minutes. Remove and soak in ice water to
　　cool, drain and slice thin.
2　Wash white part of the green onion, and cut into
　　diagonal thin slices. Rinse with cold water, pat
　　dry and arrange on top of pig ear. Pour mixture
　　2 over the pig ear and green onion. Mix well and
　　sprinkle minced coriander on the top. Serve.

煨滷牛肚
Braised Soy Tripe

牛肚(蜂巢肚1個) 約460公克
麻油 1小匙
滷汁 .... 請參見滷牛腱

1　牛肚洗淨，入開水中煮１０分鐘以去腥味，取出漂涼洗
　　淨。
2　將牛肚入煮開之滷汁中，續煮開後，改小火加蓋煮５０
　　分鐘，熄火再燜１５分鐘，撈起，待涼切絲排盤，最後
　　灑上麻油即可。

1 lb. (460 g) tripe
1 t. sesame oil
soy braising sauce
　(see "Soy Braised Beef Shank", page 73)

1　Wash tripe, place in boiling water and boil for 10
　　minutes to get rid of the odor. Remove and rinse
　　to cool.
2　Place tripe into boiled soy braising sauce and
　　bring to a boil. Cover and simmer over low heat
　　for 50 minutes. Turn off the heat and leave tripe
　　in the sauce for another 15 minutes. Remove from
　　the sauce, shred when cool. Arrange tripe shreds
　　on a plate, sprinkle with sesame oil and serve.

涼拌牛筋
Cold Beef Tendon

牛筋 .... 300公克　蔥白 35公克
香菜末 1大匙

水 8杯	醬油 2¹/₃大匙
蔥 5段	蒜末、麻油、糖各1大匙
1 薑 1片	**2** 白醋 2¹/₂小匙
醬油 2大匙	鹽 .... ¹/₄小匙
酒 1大匙	

1 牛筋洗淨，入開水中川燙，取出漂涼，再入**1**料中煮開，改小火加蓋續煮 2 ¹/₂小時（若水量不足時，需再加水，以保持水量蓋過牛筋），撈起，待涼切片備用。
2 蔥白洗淨切斜片，入冷開水中泡至稍捲後，去水瀝乾。
3 將牛筋、蔥白、**2**料及香菜拌勻即可。

■ 若牛筋不易切時，可將牛筋先冰凍一會兒，再取出切片。

---

²/₃ lb. (300 g) beef tendon
1¹/₄ oz. (35 g) green onion (white part only)
1 T. minced coriander

┌ 8 C. water
│ 5 sections green onion (1¹/₄")
1 1 slice ginger root
│ 2 T. soy sauce
└ 1 T. cooking wine

┌ 2¹/₃ T. soy sauce
│ 1 T. each: minced garlic cloves , sesame oil ,
│   sugar
2 2¹/₂ t. white vinegar
└ ¹/₄ t. salt

1 Wash beef tendon, parboil in boiling water. Remove and rinse to cool. Place in **1** and bring to a boil, cover and simmer over low heat for 2¹/₂ hours (water may be added to cover beef tendon during simmering). Remove from the pot and slice when cool.
2 Wash white part of green onion and cut into diagonal slices. Soak in cold water until the pieces curl. Drain.
3 Mix beef tendon, white part of green onion, and coriander. Season with **2** and serve.

■ To make slicing easier, tendon may be frozen slightly before slicing.

麻辣牛筋
Spicy Beef Tendon

牛筋 .... 300公克　蔥白 70公克

紅油 1¹/₂大匙	
高湯 2大匙	
1 白醋 1¹/₂小匙	
糖 1¹/₄小匙	
鹽 .... ³/₄小匙	
花椒粉、味精 各¹/₂小匙	

1 牛筋、蔥白做法請參考涼拌牛筋之做法1、2。
2 將牛筋、蔥白與**1**料拌勻即可。

---

²/₃ lb. (300 g) beef tendon
2¹/₃ oz. (70 g) green onion (white part only)

┌ 1¹/₂ T. chili oil
│ 2 T. stock
│ 1¹/₂ t. white vinegar
1 1¹/₄ t. sugar
│ ³/₄ t. salt
└ ¹/₂ t. Szechwan peppercorn powder

1 Please repeat steps 1 and 2 of "Cold Beef Tendon".
2 Mix beef tendon, green onion and **1** well. Serve.

滷牛腱
Braised Soy Beef Shank

| 牛腱 .... 600公克 | 麻油 .... 1小匙 |

1
- 水 8杯
- 酒 1大匙
- 蔥 5段
- 薑 2片

2
- 蔥段 4段
- 薑片 4片
- 蒜頭 5粒
- 紅辣椒 1條

3
- 醬油露 1¹/₄杯
- 酒 .... ¹/₂杯
- 冰糖 1²/₃大匙

4
- 花椒粒 1小匙
- 小茴 .... ¹/₄小匙
- 桂皮（拍碎）.. ¹/₈小匙
- 八角 1顆

1　牛腱洗淨，入煮開之 **1** 料內再煮開後，改小火蓋鍋續煮至湯汁剩5杯（約1小時），撈起，待涼後用叉子戳洞，湯汁則過濾去渣備用。

2　蒜頭洗淨拍碎，辣椒洗淨切成兩段， **4** 料裝入滷包袋中備用。

3　鍋熱入油2大匙燒熱，入 **2** 料爆香，續入 **3** 料、滷包袋即成滷汁，再入牛腱煮約10分鐘（煮時須經常翻面，使顏色均勻），續入牛肉湯汁煮開，改小火加蓋續煮50分鐘後，熄火燜至湯汁變涼，撈出牛腱切片排盤，上灑麻油即可。

■　若牛腱切片後中間部位味道不夠，則淋上少許牛肉滷汁後，再倒出滷汁，如此重覆數次即可。

1¹/₃ lb. (600 g) beef shank
1 t. sesame oil

1
- 8 C. water
- 1 T. cooking wine
- 5 sections green onion (1¹/₄")
- 2 slices ginger root

2
- 4 sections green onion (1¹/₄")
- 4 slices ginger root
- 5 garlic cloves
- 1 red chili pepper

3
- 1¹/₄ C. soy sauce
- ¹/₂ C. cooking wine
- 1²/₃ T. crystal sugar

4
- 1 t. Szechwan peppercorns
- ¹/₄ t. fennel
- ¹/₈ t. crushed cinnamon
- 1 star anise

1　Bring **1** to a boil and add washed beef shank. Bring to a boil again, cover and simmer over low heat until the soup reduces to 5C. (about 1 hour). Remove beef shank from the pot, pierce beef with a fork when cooled. Strain the soup until it is clear.

2　Wash peel, and crush garlic cloves. Wash red chili pepper and cut into 2 sections. Place **4** into a spice pouch.

3　Heat a wok, add 2 T. oil. Stir-fry **2** until fragrant, then add **3** and spice pouch to make soy braising sauce. Add beef shank, cook for 10 minutes (turn frequently to brown the meat evenly). Pour in the beef soup, bring to a boil. Cover and simmer over low heat for 50 minutes. Turn off the heat, leave beef in the sauce until sauce cools. Remove beef from the pot, cut into thin slices and arrange on a plate. Sprinkle sesame oil over the top and serve.

■　To strengthen flavor, pour a little sauce over the beef slices. Pour off excess sauce. Repeat the process of pouring and pouring off until desired flavor reached.

燻雞
Smoked Chicken

雞（1隻）....... 1800公克

1┌ 鹽 3大匙
　├ 花椒粒 1大匙
　└ 八角 8顆

2┌ 酒 3¹/₃大匙
　├ 蔥 5段
　└ 薑 5片

3┌ 糖 4大匙
　├ 紅茶葉 3大匙
　└ 研磨咖啡 1大匙

1 鍋熱入**1**料以小火炒黃（約5分鐘），待涼後與**2**料拌勻即為醃料。
2 雞洗淨拭乾水份，置容器內，以醃料擦遍雞身內外，蓋上保鮮膜冷藏醃1天（期間需翻身1次）。
3 雞取出，抖掉醃料，入鍋大火蒸40分鐘至雞肉全熟，待涼備用。
4 另備一鍋，鍋底鋪鋁箔紙，上置**3**料，再擺上鐵絲網或筷子，最後放上雞，加蓋以中火燻5分鐘後，改小火燻5分鐘，再熄火靜置10分鐘，打開鍋蓋刷上少許油，最後切塊排盤即可。

---

4 lb. (1800 g) chicken

1┌ **3 T. salt**
　├ **1 T. Szechwan peppercorns**
　└ **8 star anises**

2┌ **3¹/₃ T. cooking wine**
　├ **5 sections green onion (1¹/₄")**
　└ **5 slices ginger root**

3┌ **4 T. sugar**
　├ **3 T. black tea leaves**
　└ **1 T. ground coffee beans**

1 Heat a wok and stir- fry **1** over low heat until color changes to brown (about 5 minutes). Remove and cool. Mix it well with **2**, the marinating mixture.
2 Wash the chicken and pat dry. Place it in a container, rub the marinating mixture both inside and outside of chicken. Cover and refrigerate for one day, turning once mid-day.
3 Shake the marinating mixture off the chicken and steam over high heat for 40 minutes or until chicken is cooked. Remove and cool.
4 Line a wok with aluminum foil. Spread out **3** on the bottom. Place a smoking net, or use chopsticks as a rack, on top. Place the chicken on the net or the rack and cover with a lid. Smoke over medium heat for 5 minutes, then turn the heat to low and smoke for 5 minutes. Turn off the heat. Leave the chicken in the covered wok for another 10 minutes. Remove the chicken, and brush on a little oil. Cut into serving pieces and serve.

鹽酥雞
Crispy Garlic Chicken

雞胸 .... 300公克　地瓜粉 .... ¹/₂杯
胡椒鹽 1小匙

1┌ 蛋 .... ¹/₂個
　├ 醬油 1¹/₃大匙
　├ 酒、蒜末 各1大匙
　├ 糖 1小匙
　└ 鹽、五香粉 .. 各¹/₄小匙

1 雞胸肉洗淨切2×3公分塊狀，入**1**料醃20分鐘後，沾地瓜粉備用。
2 鍋熱入油4杯燒至九分熱（200℃），入雞塊以中火炸至金黃色（約2分鐘），撈起瀝油，食時沾胡椒鹽即可。

---

²/₃ lb. (300 g) chicken breast
¹/₂ C. cornstarch
1 t. pepper salt

1┌ **¹/₂ egg**
　├ **1¹/₃ T. soy sauce**
　├ **1T. each: cooking wine, minced garlic cloves**
　├ **1t. sugar**
　└ **¹/₄ t. each: salt, five-spice powder**

1 Wash chicken breast and cut into 2 x 3 cm (1" x 1") serving pieces. Marinate in **1** for 20 minutes, coat with cornstarch.
2 Heat a wok . Add 4C. oil and heat to 200°C (390°F). Deep-fry chicken breast over medium heat until color turns to golden brown (about 2 minutes). Remove from oil and drain. Sprinkle on pepper salt when serving.

棒棒雞
Bon Bon Chicken

雞胸肉 180公克	小黃瓜、粉皮 .. 各150公克
蔥末 1/2大匙	麻油 2小匙
鹽 1/2小匙	

1
- 高湯 3大匙
- 芝麻醬、麻油 各2大匙
- 白醋、醬油、辣油、蒜末 各1大匙
- 糖 2 1/2小匙
- 蠔油、花生醬 各2小匙
- 蔥末 1/2大匙
- 薑泥 1小匙

1 雞胸肉洗淨，入鍋以大火蒸熟（約10分鐘），待涼拆絲；小黃瓜洗淨切細絲，入鹽醃至軟後（約20分鐘），稍擠乾水份；粉皮入開水中川燙，撈起，以麻油拌開備用。
2 將小黃瓜置於盤底，依序放上粉皮、雞絲及蔥末，食時再拌入調勻之 **1** 料即可。

6 1/4 oz. (180 g) chicken breast
1/3 lb. (150 g) each: gherkin cucumbers,
                      mung bean sheets
1/2 T. minced green onion
2 t. sesame oil
1/2 t. salt

1
- 3 T. stock
- 2 T. each: sesame paste, sesame oil
- 1 T. each: white vinegar, soy sauce, chili oil,
           minced garlic cloves
- 2 1/2 t. sugar
- 2 t. each: oyster sauce, peanut butter
- 1/2 T. minced green onion
- 1 t. ginger roots paste

1 Wash chicken breast, steam over high heat until cooked (about 10 minutes). When cool, shred by hand. Wash cucumbers and shred. Marinate with salt until soft (about 20 minutes), pat dry. Scald mung bean sheets in boiling water, remove from the water and mix thoroughly with sesame oil.
2 Arrange shredded cucumbers on a plate, then arrange in this order mung bean sheets, shredded chicken, and minced green onion. Blend sauce **1** well, pour overall and mix well before serving.

豆腐香雞
Chicken with Tofu

雞腿（1隻）...... 300公克	硬豆腐（1塊）.... 200公克

1 蛋白 1個	**2** 鹽、味精 各1/4小匙
水 1小匙	辣椒粉 1/8小匙
鹽 1/2小匙	
麻油、味精各 .. 1/4小匙	
太白粉 1/8小匙	

1 將雞腿洗淨去骨，以刀背在肉上交叉拍打，再切成小細丁，續以 **1** 料醃10分鐘；豆腐去硬邊及皮，搗成泥狀備用。
2 鍋熱入油3大匙燒熱，入雞丁炒熟，再入豆腐泥炒勻，最後以 **2** 料調味即可。

2/3 lb. (300 g) chicken leg
7 oz. (200 g) tofu (bean curd)

1
- 1 egg white
- 1 t. water
- 1/2 t. salt
- 1/4 t. sesame oil
- 1/8 t. cornstarch

2
- 1/4 t. salt
- 1/8 t. red chili pepper powder

1 Wash chicken leg and remove the bones. Pound the meat with the back of a knife and dice. Marinate with **1** for 10 minutes. Trim off the hard edges of the tofu and mash to paste.
2 Heat a wok, add 3 T. oil. Stir-fry chicken until brown. Add mashed tofu and mix well. Season with **2** and serve.

雞凍
Chicken in Aspic

雞腿（２隻）...... 600公克　豬皮 225公克

1
水	10杯
蔥	10段
薑	3片
八角	1顆
醬油	3大匙
紹興酒	1大匙
糖	1小匙
鹽	3/4小匙

1　豬皮刮除肥油，洗淨切成１×１公分小片；雞腿洗淨，一起入開水川燙後，取出備用。
2　**1**料煮開，入雞腿及豬皮以大火煮開後，改小火加蓋燜煮１５分鐘，熄火再燜１０分鐘，取出雞腿，餘汁及豬皮繼續以小火煮至湯汁剩約２杯時（約２０分鐘），濾去豬皮，湯汁留用。
3　雞腿取肉，拆成粗條，排入模型內，再倒入湯汁，待涼置冰箱冷藏，食時扣出切片即可。

1¹/₃ lb. (600 g) 2 chicken legs
8 oz. (225 g) pork skin

1
- 10 C. water
- 10 sections green onion (1¹/₄")
- 3 slices ginger root
- 1 star anise
- 3 T. soy sauce
- 1 T. Chinese Shao-Shin wine
- 1 t. sugar
- ³/₄ t. salt

1　Scrape the lard off the pork skin. Wash and cut into 1 x 1 cm (¹/₂ " x ¹/₂ ") small slices. Wash chicken legs and parboil both pork skin and chicken legs in boiling water, remove.
2　Bring **1** to a boil, add chicken legs and pork skin slices. Cover, bring to a boil, then turn the heat down and simmer over low heat for 15 minutes. Turn off the heat and let stand for 10 more minutes. Remove the chicken legs from the wok. Continue to simmer the sauce and pork skin over low heat until sauce reduces to 2C. (about 20 minutes). Strain the sauce and discard the pork skin. Reserve the sauce for later use.
3　Remove the meat from the chicken legs, and shred by hand. Arrange the chicken meat in a mold, pour over the sauce and cool. Refrigerate until set. Invert the mold onto a plate and slice. Serve.

咖哩烤雞
Curry Roast Chicken

小雞腿 600公克

1
水	2大匙
咖哩粉、酒　各1¹/₃大匙	
麻油	1大匙
鹽	1¹/₄小匙
糖	¹/₂小匙
胡椒粉	¹/₄小匙

1　小雞腿洗淨，順著雞骨將皮及肉劃開（不可劃斷），入**1**料拌醃１小時備用。
2　烤箱預熱至２００℃，入小雞腿先烤１５分鐘，取出，刷上醃雞剩下之汁液，再入烤箱以２５０℃續烤５分鐘即可。

1¹/₃ lb. (600 g) chicken drumsticks

1
- 2 T. water
- 1¹/₃ T. each: curry powder, cooking wine
- 1 T. sesame oil
- 1¹/₄ t. salt
- ¹/₂ t. sugar
- ¹/₄ t. pepper

1　Wash chicken drumsticks, score the skin and the meat (do not cut through). Marinate in **1** for 1 hour.
2　Preheat the oven to 200°C (390°F). Roast the chicken drumsticks for 15 minutes. Remove and baste with the marinating sauce. Roast again in a 250°C (480°F) oven for 5 more minutes. Serve.

三色雞捲
Colorful Chicken Rolls

去骨雞腿肉（2隻）450公克		胡蘿蔔	40公克
四季豆 30公克		香菇	4朵

1
- 醬油 1大匙
- 酒 2小匙
- 鹽 1小匙

1　香菇洗淨泡軟去蒂，切成粗條狀；胡蘿蔔洗淨去皮亦切粗條狀；四季豆洗淨去頭尾，三者均分成 2 等份備用。

2　雞腿肉用刀背在肉面上輕剁，使筋斷肉鬆，再入**1**料醃約 2 0 分鐘後，雞皮面朝下平放，中間置上 1 份香菇、胡蘿蔔及四季豆，包捲成圓筒狀，並用牙籤固定即為雞捲，放入蒸盤中以大火蒸至熟（約 2 0 分鐘）。

3　鍋熱入油 4 杯燒至八分熱（約 1 8 0℃），入雞捲炸至金黃色後（約 2 分鐘），撈出瀝油，再切成 1 公分厚片即可。

---

1 lb. (450 g) 2 boneless chicken legs
1^1/$_3$ oz. (40 g) carrot
1 oz. (30 g) string beans
4 dried Chinese black mushrooms

1
- 1 T. soy sauce
- 2 t. cooking wine
- 1 t. salt

1　Wash dried black mushrooms, soak in water until soft and discard the stems. Wash and peel the carrot. Cut both black mushrooms and carrot into thick long strips. Wash string beans and trim off both ends. Separate all three items into 2 equal portions.

2　Gently pound the chicken meat with the back of a knife. Marinate in **1** for about 20 minutes. Spread a piece of chicken on a cutting board, skin side down, place a portion of mushrooms, carrot and string beans in the middle and roll into a cylinder. Close the opening with a toothpick. Steam over high heat until cooked (about 20 minutes).

3　Heat a wok. Add 4C. oil and heat to 180°C (350°F). Deep-fry chicken rolls until golden (about 2 minutes). Remove from the oil and drain. Cut into 1 cm (^{1}/$_2$") slices and serve.

吉利雞片
Chicken Nuggets

雞胸肉 300公克		麵包粉	^{1}/$_2$杯
麵粉 2大匙		蛋	1個

1
- 蛋 .... ^{1}/$_2$個
- 酒 .... 1 大匙
- 鹽、糖、蒜末各 ^{1}/$_2$小匙
- 胡椒粉 .... ^{1}/$_8$小匙

1　雞胸肉洗淨切片，入**1**料拌醃約 1 5 分鐘後，依序裹上麵粉、蛋液及麵包粉備用。

2　鍋熱入油 6 杯燒至六分熱（1 4 0℃），入雞片以中火炸熟且外表呈金黃色（約 1 分鐘）即可。

---

^{2}/$_3$ lb. (300 g) chicken breast
^{1}/$_2$ C. fine bread crumbs
2 T. flour
1 egg (beaten)

1
- ^{1}/$_2$ egg
- 1 T. cooking wine
- ^{1}/$_2$ t. each: salt, sugar, minced garlic cloves
- ^{1}/$_8$ t. pepper

1　Wash chicken and cut into serving slices. Marinate in **1** for 15 minutes. Coat the chicken slices with flour, then egg, then roll in fine bread crumbs.

2　Heat a wok. Add 6C. oil and heat to 140°C (280 F°). Deep-fry the nuggets over medium heat until golden (about 1 minute). Serve.

雞條豆包捲
Chicken Pouches

雞胸肉 .... 150公克　豆包（3塊）....... 120公克
四季豆、熟胡蘿蔔、新鮮香　蔥綠（12枝）....... 30公克
菇 各50公克

1「酒 1小匙
　　太白粉 .... ¹/₂小匙
　　鹽、味精 ...... 各¹/₄小匙

1　香菇洗淨泡軟去蒂，與胡蘿蔔均切條狀；四季豆去老纖
　　維洗淨，切8公分長段；香菇、四季豆、蔥綠分別入開
　　水川燙後撈起，漂涼瀝乾；雞胸肉洗淨切條狀，入**1**料
　　醃10分鐘；每塊豆包展開切成3小張備用。
2　每張豆包攤平，上置雞肉、四季豆、香菇、胡蘿蔔後再
　　捲起，並用蔥綠綁住兩端，即為豆包捲。
3　鍋熱入油4杯燒至七分熱（約160℃），入豆包捲以
　　中火炸至金黃色後撈起，每捲切成兩段，食時沾番茄醬
　　或椒鹽即可。

¹/₃ lb. (150 g) chicken breast
4¹/₄ oz. (120 g) bean curd pouch (3 pieces)
1²/₃ oz. (50 g) each: string beans, boiled carrot,
　　　　　　　　fresh black mushrooms
1 oz. (30 g) green onion (12 stalks of green parts
　　　　only for the green onion string)

1「1 t. cooking wine
　　¹/₂ t. cornstarch
　　¹/₄ t. salt

1　Wash mushrooms and discard the stems. Julienne
　　both mushrooms and carrot. Discard the tough
　　fibers of the string beans,wash and cut into 8cm
　　(2³/₄") sections. Scald mushrooms, string beans,
　　and green onions in boiling water. Remove and
　　rinse under cold water to cool, drain. Wash chick-
　　en breast and cut into strips. Marinate in **1** for 10
　　minutes. Spread out bean curd pouch and cut
　　each into 3 small pieces.
2　Spread a piece of bean curd pouch out, place
　　chicken, string beans, mushrooms, and carrot in
　　the middle and roll up. Tie each end with a green
　　onion string.
3　Heat a wok. Add 4C. oil and heat to 160 C°
　　(320 F°). Deep-fry chicken pouch over medium
　　heat until golden. Remove from the oil and drain.
　　Cut each pouch into halves. Serve with ketchup,
　　pepper salt.

黑椒雞脯
Black Pepper Chicken Steak

雞胸肉 .... 300公克　蒜末 .... ¹/₂大匙
奶油 2大匙

1「辣醬油、酒 各2小匙
　　黑胡椒粉 .... ³/₄小匙
　　鹽 .... ¹/₂小匙

1　雞胸肉洗淨用刀背交叉拍鬆，入**1**料拌醃30分鐘以
　　上。
2　鍋熱入奶油2大匙燒至溶解，入雞胸肉以中火煎至熟且
　　兩面呈金黃色後，再入蒜末炒香即可。

²/₃ lb. (300 g) chicken breast
¹/₂ T. minced garlic cloves
2 T. butter

1「2 t. each: worcestershire sauce, cooking wine
　　³/₄ t. black pepper powder
　　¹/₂ t. salt

1　Wash chicken breast and pound the meat with
　　the back of a knife. Marinate the chicken in **1** for
　　at least 30 minutes.
2　Heat a wok. Melt 2T. butter. Saute the chicken
　　until golden on both sides. Stir in minced garlic
　　cloves and fry until fragrant. Serve.

豉汁鳳足
Chicken Feet in Black Bean Sauce

雞腳 300公克		醬油 1大匙	

1
┌ 濕豆豉 1¹/₂大匙
├ 蒜末 1小匙
└ 紅辣椒末 .... ¹/₂小匙

2
┌ 水 .... ¹/₂杯
├ 糖 2小匙
├ 醬油、酒 .. 各 1 ¹/₂小匙
└ 蠔油 1小匙

3
┌ 水 1小匙
└ 太白粉 .... ¹/₂小匙

1　雞腳洗淨，切成兩段，腳掌部份再對切成兩半，入醬油醃２０分鐘。
2　鍋熱入油３杯燒至八分熱（約１８０℃），入雞腳中火炸至表皮起泡後（約５分鐘），撈起瀝油備用。
3　鍋內留油１大匙燒熱，入**1**料炒香，續入**2**料及雞腳煮開，再以**3**料勾芡，盛起置碗中，入鍋蒸至熟爛（約１小時）即可。

■　濕豆豉可以洗淨之乾豆豉取代。

²/₃ lb. (300 g) chicken feet
1 T. soy sauce

1
┌ 1¹/₂ T. wet fermented black beans
├ 1 t. minced garlic cloves
└ ¹/₂ t. minced red chili pepper

2
┌ ¹/₂ C. water
├ 2 t. sugar
├ 1¹/₂ t. each: soy sauce, cooking wine
└ 1 t. oyster sauce

3
┌ 1 t. water
└ ¹/₂ t. cornstarch

1　Wash chicken feet, chop each in half, then chop in half again. Marinate in soy sauce for 20 minutes.
2　Heat a wok. Add 3C. oil and heat to 180°C (350°F). Fry chicken feet until the skin has blistered (about 5 minutes). Remove from oil and drain.
3　Reserve 1T. oil in the wok. Stir-fry **1** until fragrant. Add **2** and chicken feet, bring to a boil and thicken with **3** . Remove to a plate and steam until tender (about 1 hour). Serve.

■　Wet fermented black beans may be replaced by washed dried fermented black beans.

雞絲沙拉
Shredded Chicken Salad

雞胸（1付） 500公克		餛飩皮（10張） 40公克	

1
┌ 西生菜絲 100公克
├ 洋蔥絲、胡蘿蔔絲 ......
└ 各40公克

2
┌ 白醋 1¹/₂大匙
├ 醬油、麻油 ... 各 1 大匙
├ 糖 .... ¹/₂大匙
└ 鹽 .... ¹/₂小匙

1　水８杯煮開，入雞胸肉煮至熟後（約２０分鐘），取出，待涼去骨切粗絲；餛飩皮亦切絲備用。
2　鍋熱入油３杯燒至八分熱（約１８０℃），入餛飩皮炸至金黃色後，撈起瀝油。
3　將雞絲、**1**料、**2**料拌勻，再灑上餛飩皮絲即可。

1 lb. (500 g) chicken breast
1¹/₃ oz. (40 g) wonton wrapper (10 pieces)

1
┌ 3¹/₂ oz. (100 g) shredded lettuce
└ 1¹/₃ oz. (40 g) each: shredded onion,
　　　　　　　　　shredded carrot

2
┌ 1¹/₂ T. white vinegar
├ 1 T. each: soy sauce, sesame oil
├ ¹/₂ T. sugar
└ ¹/₂ t. salt

1　Bring 8C. water to a boil, add chicken and cook until done (about 20 minutes). Remove from the water and cool. Remove the bones and shred. Shred the wonton wrappers for later use .
2　Heat a wok. Add 3C.oil and heat to 180°C (350°F). Deep-fry shredded wonton wrappers until golden. Remove from the oil and drain.
3　Mix shredded chicken with **1** and **2** . Sprinkle on crispy wonton wrapper shreds and serve.

蘋香雞絲
Chicken and Apple Salad

雞胸肉 150公克	蘋果 150公克
海蜇皮 100公克	香菜末 2大匙

1
冷開水 2杯
鹽 1小匙

2
白醋 1½大匙
醬油、麻油 各1大匙
蒜末 2小匙
糖 1½小匙

1 海蜇皮洗淨切細絲，泡水至軟後（約2小時），撈起，再用60℃溫開水10杯直接沖燙至捲起，續入冷開水中泡軟（約1小時）。蘋果去皮洗淨切絲，入**1**料浸泡；雞胸肉洗淨，入鍋蒸至熟（約10分鐘），取出待涼後拆絲備用。
2 將蘋果絲、海蜇皮絲分別去水瀝乾，與雞絲及**2**料拌勻醃泡1小時，最後灑上香菜末即可。

---

¹/₃ lb. (150 g) chicken breast
¹/₃ lb. (150 g) apple
3¹/₂ oz. (100 g) jelly fish
2 T. minced coriander

1
2 C. water
1 t. salt

2
1¹/₂ T. white vinegar
1 T. each: soy sauce, sesame oil
2 t. minced garlic cloves
1¹/₂ t. sugar

1 Wash jelly fish, shred and soak in water until soft (about 2 hours). Remove from water, then rinse with 10C. lukewarm water at 60°C (160°F) until jelly fish curls up. Again soak in cold water until tender (about 1 hour). Peel the apple. Wash, shred, and soak in **1**. Wash chicken breast, steam until done (about 10 minutes). Cool and shred by hand.
2 Drain the shredded apple and shredded jelly fish. Mix well with shredded chicken and **2**. Let stand for one hour. Sprinkle on minced coriander and serve.

蒜苗拌雞絲
Garlic Leek and Cold Chicken Platter

雞腿（2隻） 600公克	蒜白 90公克
香菜末 6大匙	

1
酒 2大匙
鹽 1小匙

2
醬油、麻油 各2大匙
白醋 2小匙

1 雞腿洗淨，去雞皮且順著雞骨將雞肉劃開，置蒸盤中以**1**料抹勻，再入鍋以大火蒸15分鐘，熄火續燜10分鐘，取出待涼，餘汁留用；蒜白洗淨切斜片備用。
2 雞腿去骨拆成粗絲，入蒸汁、**2**料、蒜白及香菜末拌勻即可。

1¹/₃ lb. (600 g) 1 chicken leg
3 oz. (90 g) fresh garlic (white parts only)
6 T. minced coriander

1
2 T. cooking wine
1 t. salt

2
2 T. each: soy sauce , sesame oil
2 t. white vinegar

1 Wash chicken leg, peel off the skin and snip open along the center bone. Place the chicken leg in a steamer, brush with **1** and steam over high heat for 15 minutes. Turn off the heat and let stand for 10 minutes. Remove the chicken and cool. Strain the broth for later use. Wash the fresh garlic and cut into diagonal slices.
2 Remove the bones from the chicken and shred by hand. Mix shredded chicken with the broth, **2**, fresh garlic slices, and minced coriander thoroughly. Serve.

香酥小雞腿
Finger Licking Chicken

小雞腿	600公克	蛋黃	3個
太白粉	1杯	胡椒鹽	1小匙

1
- 蔥 10段
- 薑 2片
- 醬油 .... ³/₄大匙
- 酒 .... ¹/₂大匙
- 鹽、糖 .... 各¹/₂小匙
- 味精、麻油、胡椒粉、
- 五香粉 .... 各¹/₄小匙

1　小雞腿洗淨瀝乾，入 **1** 料醃1小時後（肉厚部份用牙籤刺洞較易入味），沾裹打勻之蛋黃，再沾上太白粉備用。

2　鍋熱入油6杯燒至六分熱（約140℃），入小雞腿以小火炸至金黃色後（約10分鐘），撈起，食時再灑上胡椒鹽即可。

1¹/₃ lb. (600 g) chicken drumsticks
3 egg yolks (beaten)
1 C. cornstarch
1 t. pepper salt

1
- 10 sections green onion (1¹/₄")
- 2 slices ginger root
- ³/₄ T. soy sauce
- ¹/₂ T. cooking wine
- ¹/₂ t. each: salt, sugar
- ¹/₄ t. each: sesame oil, pepper, five-spice powder

1　Wash chicken drumsticks and drain. Marinate in **1** for 1 hour (pierce the thick part with a toothpick for the flavor to penetrate). Dip into egg yolks, then coat with cornstarch.

2　Heat a wok. Add 6C. oil and heat to 140°C (280°F). Deep-fry chicken drumsticks over low heat until golden brown (about 10 minutes). Remove from oil. Sprinkle on pepper salt during serving.

桂花鹽水鴨
Salted Duck with Osmanthus Flavor

鴨（1隻）	1700公克	鹽	500公克
八角	30公克	桂花醬	1大匙
花椒粒	¹/₂大匙		

1
- 紹興酒 1大匙
- 蔥 8段
- 薑 5片

1　鴨洗淨瀝乾水份，用叉子在鴨身上叉洞，以利調味汁之滲入。

2　鍋熱入花椒粒以小火炒30秒，再入鹽、八角、**1** 料和水30杯煮40分鐘即為白滷汁。

3　將鴨入白滷汁中煮5分鐘，再入桂花醬，熄火浸泡24小時（鴨身必須完全浸泡滷汁中），最後取出切塊即可。

3³/₄ lb. (1700 g) 1 duck
1 lb. (500 g) salt
1 oz. (30 g) star anise
1 T. osmanthus jam
¹/₂ T. Szechwan peppercorns

1
- 1 T.Chinese Sho-Shin wine
- 8 sections green onion (1¹/₄")
- 5 slices ginger root

1　Wash and pat the duck dry. Pierce the duck with a fork.

2　Heat a wok. Fry the Szechwan peppercorns over low heat for 30 seconds. Add salt, star anise, **1** , and 30C. water. Cook for 40 minutes to make the broth.

3　Cook the duck in the broth for 5 minutes. Stir in the osmanthus jam, cover and turn off the heat. Soak the duck in the broth for 24 hours (duck must be covered by the broth). Remove from the pot, cut into pieces and serve cold.

煎雞腿
Chicken Leg Pot Roast

去骨雞腿肉（2隻）450公克　蔥 5段
麻油 2大匙

1	醬油 2大匙		**2**	酒 1大匙
	麻油 1大匙			糖 2小匙
				薑汁 1小匙

1　雞腿肉用刀背在肉面上輕剁後，入**1**料醃２０分鐘取出，醃汁留用。
2　鍋熱入麻油２大匙燒熱，入蔥段爆香後撈出，續入雞腿兩面略煎，再入**2**料及醃肉餘汁，加蓋以小火燜煮１０分鐘，打開鍋蓋改中火煎至汁液收乾，取出待涼，切１公分寬斜片即可。

---

1 lb. (450 g) 2 boneless chicken legs
5 sections green onion (1^1/$_4$")
2 T. sesame oil

1 ⌈ **2 T. soy sauce**
　⌊ **1 T. sesame oil**

2 ⌈ **1 T. cooking wine**
　| **2 t. sugar**
　⌊ **1 t. ginger roots juice**

1　Gently pound the chicken meat with the back of a knife. Marinate in **1** for 20 minutes. Remove the chicken and save the marinating sauce for later use.
2　Heat a wok. Add 2T. sesame oil and stir-fry green onion sections until fragrant. Discard the green onion sections. Add chicken and lightly saute on both sides, pour in **2** and marinating sauce. Cover and simmer over low heat for 10 minutes. Remove the lid and turn heat to medium. Continue cooking until the sauce completely evaporates. Remove the chicken and cool. Cut into 1 cm(^{1}/$_2$") thick slices and serve.

醉雞
Drunken Chicken

雞腿（2隻）...... 600公克

1	蔥 12段		**2**	雞湯 3杯
	薑 5片			紹興酒 1杯
	鹽 2大匙			蝦油 2大匙
				鹽、胡椒粉 .. 各^1/$_4$小匙

1　雞腿洗淨，以**1**料抹勻醃１５分鐘；水7杯煮開，將醃好的雞腿入鍋煮１０分鐘後，熄火浸泡１５分鐘取出。
2　取一容器，將雞腿及**2**料放入（湯汁須蓋過雞腿），蓋上保鮮膜入冰箱冷藏，隔日取出切塊即可。

1^1/$_3$ lb. (600 g) 2 chicken legs

1 ⌈ **12 sections green onion (1^1/$_4$")**
　| **5 slices ginger root**
　⌊ **2 T. salt**

2 ⌈ **3 C. Chicken stock**
　| **1 C. Chinese Shao- Shin wine**
　| **2 T. shrimp oil**
　⌊ **^{1}/$_4$ t. each: salt, pepper**

1　Wash the chicken legs. Marinate in **1** for 15 minutes. Bring 7C. water to a boil in a pot, add the marinated chicken legs. Cook for 10 minutes, remove from heat and let stand for 15 minutes. Remove the chicken legs from the pot.
2　Place the chicken legs and **2** in a deep container (the liquid must cover the chicken legs). Cover with plastic wrap and keep in refrigerator overnight. Cut into serving pieces the next day. Serve cold.

杭州醬鴨
Hangchow Marinated Duck

鴨（１隻）.......１８００公克
淺色醬油 ４杯
鹽.............................. ２大匙
紹興酒 １大匙
糖........................... $^1/_2$大匙
蔥.............................. ３段
薑.............................. ２片
硝....................... ０.１８公克

1 鴨洗淨去鴨掌，用小鐵鉤勾住鴨鼻孔，掛在通風處風乾水份（ 約２小時）。
2 將鹽和硝拌勻，在鴨身內外抹勻後，將鴨頭扭向胸前挾在右腋下，平整地放進長方形保鮮盒內，蓋好再放入冰箱冷藏，醃１ $^1/_2$ 天後，翻身再醃１ $^1/_2$ 天即可取出，倒掉汁液。
3 鴨放入保鮮盒內入醬油浸泡，加蓋再放入冰箱冷藏浸泡２天後，翻身再浸泡２天，取出，剖開腹部，用兩枝竹筷子，從腹部刀口處塞入肚內，使腹腔向兩側敞開。
4 將醃鴨的醬油倒入鍋中煮開，入鴨並用湯杓將醬油徐徐淋在鴨身上，至呈暗紅色後撈起，置通風處風乾２天。
5 醬鴨放在大盤子上，灑上糖、蔥段、薑片及紹興酒，入鍋大火蒸２０分鐘，冷卻後切塊裝盤即可。

■ 由於硝用量受限制，且量太少不易秤量，因此最好取硝 $^1/_4$ 小匙分成７等份，取其中１份即為１隻鴨的硝用量。

---

4 lb. (1800 g) 1 duck
4 C. light brown soy sauce
2 T. salt
1 T. Chinese Shao-Shin wine
$^1/_2$ T. sugar
3 sections green onion (1$^1/_4$")
2 slices ginger root
0.18 g sodium nitrite

1 Wash the duck and cut off the duck feet. Hang the duck from an iron hook, and air-dry for about 2 hours.
2 Mix the salt and sodium nitrite well, rub the inside and the outside of the duck with the mixture. Twist the duck head under the right wing . Place the duck in an air-tight container, cover, and refrigerate for 1$^1/_2$ days. Turn the duck and marinate for another 1$^1/_2$ days. Remove; discard the liquid.
3 Soak the duck in the soy sauce in an air tight container. Refrigerate for 2 more days. Turn the duck and soak for another 2 days, remove. Cut open the cavity of the duck, insert a pair of bamboo chopsticks in the cavity and split open into two halves .
4 Bring the soy sauce for marinating the duck to a boil. Add the duck and spoon sauce onto duck constantly until the color turns dark red. Remove and air-dry for 2 days.
5 Place the duck on a big plate. Sprinkle with sugar, green onions, ginger, and Chinese Shao-Shin wine. Steam over high heat for 20 minutes. Cool and cut into serving pieces. Arrange on a plate and serve.

■ The amount of sodium nitrite used is very little and difficult to weigh. Therefore, divide $^1/_4$ t. sodium nitrite into 7 equal portions. Use one portion for one duck.

More Wei-Chuan Cook Books

純青出版社

劃撥帳號：12106299

地址：台北市松江路125號4樓

電話：（02）2508-4331
　　　　　　　 2506-3564

傳真：（02）2507-4902

Distributor: Wei-Chuan Publishing

1455 Monterey Pass Rd., #110
Monterey Park, CA 91754, U.S.A.
Tel: (323)2613880・2613878
Fax: (323)2613299

家常菜
- 226道菜
- 200頁
- 中文版

健康食譜
- 100道菜
- 120頁
- 中英對照

Healthful Cooking
- 100 recipes
- 120 pages
- Chinese/English Bilingual

素食
- 84道菜
- 120頁
- 中英對照

Vegetarian Cooking
- 84 recipes
- 120 pages
- Chinese/English Bilingual

健康素
- 76道菜
- 96頁
- 中英對照

Simply Vegetarian
- 76 recipes
- 96 pages
- Chinese/English Bilingual

微波食譜第一冊
- 62道菜
- 112頁
- 中英對照

Microwave Cooking Chinese Style
- 62 recipes
- 112 pages
- Chinese/English Bilingual

微波食譜第二冊
- 76道菜
- 128頁
- 中英對照

Microwave Cooking Chinese Style 2
- 76 recipes
- 128 pages
- Chinese/English Bilingual

養生家常菜
- 80道菜
- 96頁
- 中英對照

Chinese Home Cooking for Health
- 80 recipes
- 96 pages
- Chinese/English Bilingual

實用烘焙
- 77道點心
- 96頁
- 中英對照

International Baking Delight
- 77 recipes
- 96 pages
- Chinese/English Bilingual

飲茶食譜
- 88道菜
- 128頁
- 中英對照

Chinese Dim Sum
- 88 recipes
- 128 pages
- Chinese/English Bilingual

養生藥膳
- 73道菜
- 128頁
- 中英對照

Chinese Herb Cooking for Health
- 73 recipes
- 128 pages
- Chinese/English Bilingual

廣東菜
- 75道菜
- 96頁
- 中英對照

Chinese Cuisine Cantonese Style
- 75 recipes
- 96 pages
- Chinese/English Bilingual

營養便當
- 147道菜
- 96頁
- 中文版

嬰幼兒食譜
- 140道菜
- 104頁
- 中文版

無油煙食譜
- 46道菜
- 68頁/菊16開
- 中文版

快手菜食譜
- 49道菜
- 68頁/菊16開
- 中文版

美容餐食譜
- 50道菜
- 68頁/菊16開
- 中文版

米食-家常篇
- 84道菜
- 96頁
- 中英對照

米食-傳統篇
- 82道菜
- 96頁
- 中英對照

麵食-家常篇
- 91道菜
- 96頁
- 中英對照

麵食-精華篇
- 87道菜
- 96頁
- 中英對照

美味小菜
- 92道菜
- 96頁
- 中英對照

Rice
Home Cooking
- 84 recipes
- 96 pages
- Chinese/English Bilingual

Rice
Traditional Cooking
- 82 recipes
- 96 pages
- Chinese/English Bilingual

Noodles
Home Cooking
- 91 recipes
- 96 pages
- Chinese/English Bilingual

Noodles
Classical Cooking
- 87 recipes
- 96 pages
- Chinese/English Bilingual

Appetizers
- 92 recipes
- 96 pages
- Chinese/English Bilingual

四川菜
- 115道菜
- 96頁
- 中英對照

上海菜
- 91道菜
- 96頁
- 中英對照

台灣菜
- 73道菜
- 120頁
- 中英對照

庖廚偏方 庖廚錦囊 庖廚樂
- 中文版

Chinese Cuisine
Szechwan Style
- 115 recipes
- 96 pages
- Chinese/English Bilingual

Chinese Cuisine
Shanghai Style
- 91 recipes
- 96 pages
- Chinese/English Bilingual

Chinese Cuisine
Taiwanese Style
- 73 recipes
- 120 pages
- Chinese/English Bilingual

味全家政班

味全家政班創立於民國五十年，經過三十餘年的努力，它不只是國內歷史最悠久的家政研習班，更成為一所正式學制之外的專門學校。

創立之初，味全家政班以教授中國菜及研習烹飪技術為主，因教學成果良好，備受各界讚譽，乃於民國五十二年，增闢插花、工藝、美容等各門專科，精湛的師資，教學內容的充實，深獲海內外的肯定與好評。

三十餘年來，先後來班參與研習的學員已近二十萬人次，學員的足跡遍及台灣以外，更有許多國外的團體或個人專程抵台，到味全家政班求教，在習得中國菜烹調的精髓後，或返回居住地經營餐飲業，或擔任家政教師，或獲聘為中國餐廳主廚者大有人在，成就倍受激賞。

近年來，味全家政班亟力研究開發改良中國菜餚，並深入國際間，採集各種精緻、道地美食，除了樹立中華文化「食的精神」外，並將各國烹飪口味去蕪存菁，擷取地方特色。為了確保這些研究工作更加落實，我們特將這些集合海內外餐飲界與研發單位的精典之作，以縝密的拍攝技巧與專業編輯，出版各式食譜，以做傳承。

薪傳與發揚中國烹飪的藝術，是味全家政班一貫的理念，日後，也將秉持宗旨，永續不輟。

Wei-Chuan
Cooking School

Since its establishment in 1961, Wei-Chuan Cooking School has made a continuous commitment toward improving and modernizing the culinary art of cooking and special skills training. As a result, it is the oldest and most successful school of its kind in Taiwan.

In the beginning, Wei-Chuan Cooking School was primarily teaching and researching Chinese cooking techniques. However, due to popular demand, the curriculum was expanded to cover coureses in flower arrangements, handcrafts, beauty care, dress making and many other specialized fields by 1963.

The fact that almost 200,000 students, from Taiwan and other countries all over the world, have matriculated in this school can be directly attributed to the high quality of the teaching staff and the excellent curriculum provided to the students. Many of the graduates have become successful restaurant owners and chefs, and in numerous cases, respected teachers.

While Wei-Chuan Cooking School has always been committed to developing and improving Chinese cuisine, we have recently extended our efforts toward gathering information and researching recipes from different provinces of China. With the same dedication to accuracy and perfection as always, we have begun to publish these authentic regional gourmet recipes for our devoted readers. These new publications will continue to reflect the fine tradition of quality our public has grown to appreciate and expect.